Lake Nation

People and the Fate
of the Great Lakes

Dave Dempsey

DEDICATION

To Lana Pollack
Fearless champion of the Great Lakes
And a just society

Introduction

This is not a book about the Great Lakes themselves, although the Great Lakes figure prominently in the story.

Instead, this is a book seeking to understand something about the people who love the Great Lakes – the Lake Nation – and their relationship to those lakes. Estimated at roughly 35 million, the population of the Canadian and American Great Lakes watershed is greater than that of Saudi Arabia, Australia or Taiwan. If this population formally constituted a nation, it would be approximately the 40th largest in the world. Thirty-five million is a lot of people, and it's a lot of impact on the world's largest freshwater ecosystem.

Therein lies the story. These many millions flush their wastes, fertilize their lawns or farms, use electricity, drive their vehicles and buy things, lots of things. In all of these activities they – we, for I'm one – place burdens on the Great Lakes.

But at the same time, for millions among them, the Great Lakes touch what Lincoln (by way of Seward) called "the mystic chords of memory." The Lakes represent carefree beach holidays of youth, charter fishing trips that resulted in the catch of a prize salmon, the calm rhythm of waves heard at night from a cabin in the coastal woods, the limitless vista from atop a dune. These are not meaningless fragments lodged in the mind. They are experiences attached to emotions, and one of these emotions is love.

We say we love them. So why are the Great Lakes so at risk? Why don't we love them enough to protect them? Shedding my public policy orientation, I decided to go right into the heart of the question, the hearts of people who know the Lakes. I make no pretense that this is a scientific study or a statistically valid sample of the Great Lakes populace. I interviewed people I know, some for decades, some for a year, some as intimate friends, some as contacts. I wanted to collect impressions and ideas. I leave it to others to do more rigorous analysis.

I wanted to hear stories, and I wanted to divine some lessons.

Prelude

On summer evenings I've several times joined a mass pedestrian migration in South Haven, Michigan. A typical experience goes like this: As the sun wheels toward the west northwest an hour before sunset, hundreds of people stroll down to the two beaches and piers that serve as shoulders for the Black River as it offers its gift of water to the majesty of Lake Michigan. The minutes pass, and the piers grow dense with the expectant. The orange-red sun descends with dignity through a transparent screen of yellow cirrus clouds. The green-blue waters of the fourth-largest lake in the world prepare to receive the orb. Except for the cries of playing children, a general hush descends as the day nears its end.

Among the multitude are vacationers and locals, environmentalists and business moguls, Democrats and Republicans, young couples, families and retirees. There are native Michiganders and tourists from distant states and nations. There are no arguments. A sense of wonder at the arching sky and expansive fresh water prevails.

The sun makes contact with the liquid horizon, and the crowd murmurs its admiration. Some raise their smartphones in an unconscious salute, trying to capture a moment whose associated emotions elude even the most astute camera. Couples cling, smiling and exclaiming. Even the children stop their play to watch in awe as the sun's lower half flattens against the water.

Now the sun is poised to offer its final performance of the day. It is a regal eminence, then a red bubble, finally a mischievous child's eye taking one last peek back at the thousands of eyes studying it. Then, the water takes it in.

The light immediately changes, dims slightly. But the water is unchanged. It snaps rhythmically against the piers. Power boats, cruisers and compact motorboats begin flocking back to shore, chugging their way through the channel toward their berths. Their occupants wave and smile at the crowds on the piers. Sailboats, even a kayak or two join them on their return.

The many who have savored this spectacle turn their backs – often reluctantly – on the lake to return to South Haven, or to vehicles that may carry them many miles inland before they sleep. They've satisfied a craving for primal beauty, for something bigger and more enduring than themselves – something intertwined with one of North America's Great Lakes. They're united in admiration. It's a ritual that is repeated night, after summer night.

In government conference rooms across the region, a different sort of ritual is repeated as public servants, green advocates, business interests and others convene to debate and shape the policies intended to protect the lakes. At such a gathering in Toronto in October 2016, U.S. and Canadian scientists discussed a report concluding, "Overall, the 2016 state of the Great Lakes is Fair and Unchanging." Lake Superior was deemed in good condition, Lakes Michigan, Huron and Ontario in fair condition, and Lake Erie in poor condition. No lake was graded as attaining all of the objectives set for it in domestic law or international agreement. The self-assessment of the governments was that things were so-so.

Many of the people of this region would not agree with them.

Things were not "so-so" in Toledo, Ohio in August 2014, when city officials told them not to use the public drinking water supply for nearly three days because of a toxin generated in Lake Erie that was ultimately attributable to phosphorus pollution.

Things were not "so-so" if they lived along the Kalamazoo River near Marshall, Michigan in August 2010 and they watched oil spilled from a ruptured pipeline snaking along the waterway, menacing fish and wildlife and requiring a cleanup costing more than $1 billion.

Things were not "so-so" for anglers almost anywhere in the Great Lakes system, with health agencies cautioning them to limit what they eat of their catch because of mercury, PCBs and other pollutants banned long ago – but still riding in the bodies of aquatic organisms.

Things were not "so-so" for anyone worried about the microplastic particles that abound in the Great Lakes, the spent nuclear fuel stored on their shores, the wetlands of the Great Lakes system devoured for development, the new chemicals turning up in their fish and wildlife, the approaching Asian carp, the mushrooming impacts of climate change, and on and on.

In spite of this, there are signs of hope: the cleanup of old toxic hotspots, the reclamation of beaches, and the recovery of urban waterfronts. Often unheralded, people are working to protect their share of the Great Lakes in scores of communities in Canada and the U.S.

But it's not enough.

The Great Lakes aren't dying, but they're in trouble. They are not "so-so." Perhaps they're always in trouble, but that only reinforces the question: when so many love them, when a monumental majority say they want the lakes protected, when polls, focus groups and informal surveys document almost infinitesimally small minorities who don't care, how can the Lakes be struggling? Why are they at risk?

As a lifelong political practitioner, my first impulse is to ask why overwhelming public sentiment doesn't rescue the lakes. Some might take the easy out and blame a crumbling system of governance – but some old rules still apply to that system. A clamoring public, although infrequently aroused en masse these days, still mostly gets what it wants.

Combined into a powerful coalition, the sunset watchers,

lighthouse lovers, sport anglers, freighter nerds, passionate boaters, devoted swimmers and most of all, drinking water consumers should be able to effect any policy they want. But they *aren't* combined into a powerful coalition. They often barely take note of each other, like pedestrians brushing past each other on a Chicago street.

I wonder whether we have enough in common to effect a transformation.

Chapter 1

Karen Norton showed up when I needed her. After moving to a location near Port Huron, Michigan in the late summer of 2015, I had several urgent arrangements to make with help from an unfamiliar community. A good dog sitter was one of them.

My living companion was a 16-pound Morkie (Yorkie/Maltese mix) named Fitz, after F. Scott Fitzgerald, my favorite author. A generally happy canine with a tendency to fixate on birds, squirrels and bicyclists, he would need watching when I traveled, usually for business. Karen's name was one provided by an internet pet sitting registry, and I asked her to come over.

She did so on a scalding hot day, with the little cottage only half-furnished and lacking an air conditioner. I was afraid I'd stick to my chair when it was time for her to leave. But if Karen noticed, she didn't mind. She was hired – in my mind – in less than two minutes even though our chat lasted nearly a half hour. Pet owners know. Dogs know. Fitz and I agreed she was not only likable, but also highly qualified. She owned dogs and adored dogs and she was kind.

Over the months that snap judgment proved correct. Fitz was sometimes more demonstrative about his excitement to see her than about my everyday presence or even my return from the office or gym.

Karen had the kindly manner of many Michiganders, those who mean it when they tell you to have a nice day, open the door for you and wait at a store, and from behind their steering wheel wave you across a pedestrian walkway in the mall parking lot. She seemed a good person to interview. She would answer my questions without guile.

Having grown up in Roseville, a northeastern suburb of Detroit, she recalled riding with her family into the city on Sundays and out to Belle Isle in the Detroit River. "That was my first experience crossing over water on a bridge to an island. We went all seasons of the year. So the river was an ever-changing, beautiful waterway. Those were very calming and there were happy family times."

She added, "even at that age, I remember seeing this beauty and feeling how lucky I was to live here."

Karen lived with her three dogs across the road from Lake Huron. I was curious how often she paid attention to the lake. I've met more than a few people who became immune to the charms of the Great Lakes after living close to them for years. She said she noticed the lake daily out her living room window. But that wasn't all. She sunbathed, watched boats, walked her dogs on a boardwalk under a bridge leading to the lake and followed the ice in the wintertime. So on a scale of Great Lakes use, she probably stood on the middle.

Did she care about the Great Lakes or just Lake Huron? First, she said she had seen only four of the Lakes – not Superior. Others she had seen chiefly while driving past. "I'm probably more concerned about Lake Huron."

I moved in to ask the questions a policy wonk wants answered. How important did she think it was to protect the Great Lakes. Very. Why? "Millions of people depend on them for drinking water." She said they were also important for fish production, wildlife habitat, and a migratory route for birds.

Did she think the lakes were improving or deteriorating? "Oh, they're getting worse," she said. She ticked off a list of threats longer than most people can compile: invasive species, toxic pollution, wetland destruction, sewage overflows, and climate change. I asked her to identify the number one threat to the Lakes and she gave me several number ones: mercury emissions from coal burning power plants, the risk of oil spills from pipelines, excessive nutrients from farm runoff among them. Thinking of mercury contamination, I asked whether she thought people should feel safe consuming Great Lakes fish. "No – I would *not* eat them," she said.

Did she think individuals could do anything to benefit the Great Lakes? Sure. Unlike others, who talked about recycling or buffer strips on their property, Karen said people could support projects that protect Great Lakes habitat.

I wasn't surprised when Karen said she was optimistic about the future of the Great Lakes. The Great Lakes Restoration Initiative – a name I thought only government insiders and advocates knew – was improving the health of the Lakes. Still, in the end, she said that people are responsible for the welfare of the Great Lakes. "And we need to elect the best government officials for the job."

An answer that would gladden any wonk's heart.

It was a good start. Now I would refine my questions and interview as many people as I could find that were willing to talk to me.

Interlude 1

Five miles north of Port Huron, Michigan, it's easy to see passing freighters. The east and west shores of Lake Huron converge just southward, funneling vessels into the St. Clair River (from which northbound vessels push into the lake). The shipping lane runs only a couple of miles offshore. A good pair of binoculars makes vessel identification easier, although websites, boatnerd.com and marinetraffic.com, which track freighter passage, are always available on your laptop or smartphone.

I moved to my freighter vantage point in the late summer of 2015. Renting a small cottage set back 500 feet from the lake, with the landlord's house in between, I was an inhabitant of the Great Lakes coastal zone rather than a visitor for the first time in my nearly 59 years. I had loved the Lakes as far back as I could remember, but now I would get to know one of them intimately.

I had long loved traveling west across Lower Michigan to behold sunsets. Now I was on the sunrise side. Lake Michigan was familiar, friendly, accessible. Huron had always struck me as obscure, enigmatic, colorless.

The neighborhood I joined was redolent of family summers on the lake, its cottages crammed with the old set of dishes from back home, photos of seasons past, coffee mugs of different sizes and forgotten histories, unmatched chairs around the dining room table and the musty old couch. Most of the housing was a scattering of old styles and structures — wood, stone, cinder block. It was a place where everyone got along, and there seemed little to no judgment. We had the lake in common.

One hundred miles downstream, in western Lake Erie, toxic algal blooms were once again disfiguring the waters that August. But the pool of southern Lake Huron I could see was largely free of algae and appealing to the eye. The only hindrances to a day's swimming were the bands of underwater rocks characteristic of Huron that separated beach from deeper water.

Among those rocks, I soon found out, were Petoskeys, the official state stone. Featuring coral markings imprinted in an ancient sea, the rocks are a piece of Michigan's heritage. Beachcombers eagerly seek them and often put them in water-filled jars, where their markings are more evident. I had thought Petoskeys were confined to the far north of Michigan.

Freighters captured my attention immediately. Despite their balance sheet functions, there is something romantic about them. I trace my sense of their mystique to a painting that hung on the walls of my childhood home, an heirloom descended through my mother's side of the family. The vantage point is looking out from a dune. On the horizon a tiny freighter is visible, a feather of smoke trailing behind. As a child you want to know: Who is on that ship? Where is it going? What adventures has it enjoyed, and what challenges await?

Now I was repeating those early questions as I stood looking day, evening and night.

Viewing freighters after dark awakens the imagination. Technology may have rendered life on these vessels safer and less arduous, but from land they look as vulnerable as they ever have. Through the distance their lights appear to tremble rather than twinkle. The vast waters dwarf them. The darkness over the unpopulated north of Lake Huron to the north (left from my vantage point) seems to menace them. It's a strange beauty. But it's enough to lure me outside even in severe cold.

Having worked on environmental policy most of my adult life, I'm aware that freighters are not benign. Before controls were legislated, their ballast tanks introduced a dysfunctional community of non-native aquatic organisms that transformed the Great Lakes food web. They discharge oil. Their deck sweepings end up in the water. They emit fumes. I know all that, but the sight of them returns me to an age when I felt the emotional impact, rather than the environmental impact.

I watched attentively the interplay of freighters and weather that first autumn on Lake Huron. Once, when a gale roared, eight of them anchored in the relatively confined area viewable from the beach out back. On the spectacular still and warm days, they slid north and south untroubled.

I waited for them to cease their passage as autumn became winter. They kept coming. Early winter was mild, and even on Christmas Day there was virtually no lake ice. The Soo Locks, connecting freighters with the taconite and grain stores of Duluth, closed in mid-January and the vessels persisted. It wasn't until the last week of January that they completely vanished. Saying goodbye to them for the season was less solemn with the knowledge that within 60 days they might resume.

The absence of ice enabled the lake to twitch restlessly well into the new year. From September to early February, waters hammered the shore regularly, sometimes for three or four nights in a row. I could feel the impact of the waves even lying in bed. Depending on my mood, I heard their wild rhythm as a display of strength or as the beat of anxiety.

I now learned to appreciate sunrises over Huron. I couldn't help but view them as sunsets in reverse: the silver and blue stripes of light above the horizon coming first rather than last, the sun lifting itself up over the horizon instead of easing into it. The beauty was identical.

The ice came — and went. For a brief time in mid-February the air chilled, the wind calmed, and glaze coated the lake to the horizon. Then the south wind warmed the atmosphere, thawing most of the ice and shoving the rest against the shore.

Songbirds began to carry on. Geese wailed overhead. The lake shivered blue. The cycle was continuing. I felt suspense about what would come next.

Chapter 2

I had heard of Marvin Roberson for 20 years, and conducted this interview with him, before I met him. A forest policy specialist who began working for the Michigan Chapter of the Sierra Club in 1994, Marvin was legendary for leading the fight, and often being the only fighter or one of the few, against increasingly regressive state forest policies. I began to communicate with him on a deeper level in the spring of 2016, when a friend who knew of our common health problem provided each of us the other's email address. He readily consented to answering my Great Lakes questions.

Born in Flint, Marvin was 55 at the time I interviewed him by email. In childhood, his family had owned a cabin on Higgins Lake (and still did in 2016). In his response to me, he said that experience "helped shape my perception of Michigan as a water-based area, even though we were not on one of the Great Lakes. Partly because of the cottage, and partly because of the Lakes, it was not until college years that I truly realized that not everyone has seemingly unlimited water mere minutes away."

Marvin had one of the more striking job histories of anyone I interviewed: he'd driven beer trucks, been a groundskeeper, served as a mental health professional, managed the historic Calumet Theater, and for the previous 20 years had been a professional forest ecologist.

His childhood awareness of the Great Lakes, he said, seemed to reach back to a family driving trip through Michigan and Wisconsin. "We crossed Lake Michigan on the *Badger* back when it was a working rail ferry, before it turned into a tourist boat. I was awed at the notion that trains got on a boat, and crossed a Great Lake. At each motel, almost all of them waterfront, my sister and I would immediately run into the water out front. I remember the shock at discovering that Lake Superior was not warm and forgiving, like the others, but frigid and kinda scary."

Not long before the interview he had traveled to Isle Royale for "some park planning business, after the season was over. I got to spend a week in a Park Service cabin, all to myself, right on the shore. I've been to Isle Royale many times, but this was the most magical." His relationship to Lake Superior was intimate: he saw it every day.

With his next answer, Marvin confirmed his fitness for the title Old Man of the North Woods, although he wasn't that old yet. I asked him if he cared more about one Great Lake than another. His answer: "Superior - remote, cold, harsh, and north have always called to me."

He said Superior came up frequently with friends: "How it looks is a part of everyday conversation, as well as which, if any, freighters are in." The politics of the Great Lakes did not.

I asked him to sum up his feelings about the Great Lakes in one sentence, then in one word. "I can appreciate other areas, but every time I travel, I start to yearn for the green and blue of Michigan and its lakes. One word? Cool."

Marvin wasn't the only one to question my use of the word "protect" when I asked him: how important is it to protect the Lakes? "The phrase 'protect the Great Lakes' can mean a myriad of things, and gets bandied about in a dozen different contexts, not all of which are consistent with one another."

Did he think the Great Lakes were getting better, worse or staying about the same? "All of the above. Better - less discharges, more scrutiny. Worse - pushes to roll back standards, diversion allowances -- both direct diversion and indirect, such as bottled water."

The greatest threat to the health of the Great Lakes, he said, was systemic in the governance system. Hundreds of overlapping, inconsistent local and state and federal jurisdictions all have the ability to allow degradation individually, he said.

A related problem was that no one had taken lead responsibility for the Lakes. "I think that Michigan's governors have great opportunities to do so, but they haven't always stepped up. Michigan has most of the shoreline, most of the basin, most of the local units, and the moral opportunity to take the lead."

By now I knew I could count him to take a contrarian view on the role of the individual. He said focusing on individual stewardship actions was far from enough. "I think that individuals pushing for institutional reforms, standards to which we must all conform, is more effective than simply voluntarily saving water, for instance, which does not mean we shouldn't take those actions. I just find that time is better spent influencing policy."

Just weeks before the 2016 presidential election he saw reason for both optimism and pessimism about the Great Lakes in the campaign. "We are very likely to elect the first woman president, who is likely the most competent, prepared, qualified individual to run in our lifetime. Meanwhile, 40% of the country is likely to vote for an ignorant, misogynist, racist bully who discusses dick size in a Presidential debate, and they will do so not in spite of those qualities, but because of them. That makes me both hopeful and pessimistic about everything."

Now, the key question: why did he think the health of the Great Lakes was questionable when so many people professed to care about them? Most people agreed on protecting the environment, he said, but the issue was relatively low on their priority list and didn't much influence their voting patterns.

"Seeing Lake Superior daily is why I put up with bugs, snow, -20 temps, and neighbors with signs like the [pro-Trump] picture I sent you," Marvin said.

A few weeks later, of course, reality pulverized our election expectations.

Interlude 2

Spring came grudgingly to the shores of Lake Huron. A mild winter yielded to a sometimes-frigid spring. A sticking snow fell in mid-April. Ice pellets stung the face in mid-May. Finally, just after the ensuing frost, the trees leafed out fully. It seemed quite late.

Winter at any latitude north of the Ohio River is a trial of the soul. In the Lake Nation, citizenship requires stoicism when the lake effect brings cloudy skies day after day. Counting the extra minute of daylight as one year turns into another is a ritual of mine. What's one minute? Well, what's one recycled bottle? It's a start.

Lake Huron was patient. Ice clotted the creeks and drains that ordinarily contribute to it, but they would soon resume their flow; of course, they were already flowing under winter's glassy surface.

Lake Huron was resilient. A storm would thrash it, but a day or two later, the lake would rest contentedly, a match for any tempest.

Lake Huron was a changeling. One day the blue of a child's lake drawing, one morning silver; one day muddy brown, one evening gold.

Lake Huron was ready for spring. The signal of hope whose memory persisted even in the harrowing weather of April was the lake's behavior one Sunday in March. As day began, a sheen of ice, thin but sprawling, covered much of the water. On the shores, a powdered donut kind of snow glittered in the morning sun. Then the wind shifted to the south. The sun assumed power high in the sky. By noon the lake ice was fractured, shriveling. By mid-afternoon it was gone. It was possible to walk down to the beach comfortably with a sweater, no jacket. The lake was quiet, softly panting, like my little dog beside me, waiting for a command, but more than happy to frolic free.

Lake Huron was just – there. I was glad.

Chapter 3

I knew my cousin by marriage, Nan Casey – an effervescent woman not shy about expressing her opinion – would have something to say about the Great Lakes. A successful attorney, she brought to our family gatherings her verbal gifts as well as a bluntness that could startle you and a sense of humor that could convulse you with laughter. She had mentioned to me being born in Petoskey, on Little Traverse Bay, so she knew the water.

"My first memory of Lake Michigan is swimming in the lake and I loved it," she said. "I was at a sheltered beach in Harbor Springs. I was about 5 years old and I felt safe and loved the water, beach, stones and sand. A couple of years later, a boat that some of my friends' fathers were in went out to Beaver Island and didn't return. They all died.

"The men who died had families. In fact, two had teens that were friends of my sister's and mine. In all, 8 children were fatherless after that night. It was a very long couple of days waiting for the bodies to be recovered and the funerals to be held. It was a memory I will never forget. To this day, chills run down my spine when I think of the memory of that terrible storm and the many lives impacted by Lake Michigan. I will never forget the fact that the Lake can turn from a quiet calm body of beautiful water to a place of surging waves and death. There wasn't the ability back then to predict the weather as there is now -- which is another way in which we have -- fortunately -- used some of our resources to protect not only property but also life.

"It led to a lifelong appreciation of the beauty of the Great Lakes, but (also) the fact they were to be feared for their ability to change quickly and ferociously."

She contrasted the childhood memory with a memory of the late August day before she sat down to answer my questions. "We walked the beach at Petoskey State Park and enjoyed the wind, sand, sun and waves. The water was choppy with whitecaps. There weren't many people on the beach and it was free of dead fish and a lot of debris. Where children were present, they were in the water playing in the waves. Some scoured the shores for Petoskey stones."

It sounded like the kind of sweet memory I had heard almost every resident of the region carry around over years and decades. Whether from yesterday or 50 years ago, these memories are sustenance – the fuel to carry on, to believe in the future and to feel rooted in a place.

Perhaps that intensity of relationship led her to declare flatly, "the Great Lakes are getting worse." She ticked off the threats she knew of from news coverage: Asian carp, polluted water in general and the algae issues arising again in Lake Erie.

Nan also observed, "I don't think enough people are concerned about the fact that the Great Lakes are so much of our clean water supply and we aren't protecting them.

On the one hand, Nan said people could help by preventing and cleaning up trash in or around the lakes. And she made the political connection: she suggested voting for candidates who will protect the Great Lakes. On the other hand, she expressed pessimism, based on skepticism about the political system and the public itself. "The legislation necessary to protect the Lakes hasn't been passed and the public appears apathetic to doing what is necessary."

She added: "I think people are selfish and don't want to make the sacrifices that are necessary to protect the lakes and they don't want to be inconvenienced or authorize the increase in taxes for some of the necessary research and changes."

But the Lakes themselves remain inspirational.

"It's been one of the greatest blessings of my life to grow up on Lake Michigan and to return there for my retirement years. I have lived in Maui and traveled to Greece, Turkey and numerous locations and I haven't found any place with the beauty of the Great Lakes. I'm grateful that I can end my life where I began it. Nothing gives me the sense of peace and contentment that being near Lake Michigan does."

A pattern was beginning to reveal itself. The lakes provide comfort and hope. The intertwined systems of politics and government provide disillusionment about the future of the lakes.

The other part of the pattern was a little surprising: an at least equal risk arises from the people who live among the lakes.

Interlude 3

I am as accomplished an outdoorsman as I am a handyman. That I have difficulty wielding a tape measure competently, let alone figuring out the intricacies of assembling a new vacuum, tells you everything you need to know about my first solitary camping experience.

It was the summer of 1993. I was 36 years old. An environmental professional for 11 years, I decided it was time to prove to myself that I was worthy of the name – that I was more than an armchair environmentalist. I wanted to show myself that I could handle the simple mechanics of inhabiting the outdoors without the help of the sympathetic friends who had always assisted me in setting up a tent or cooking dinner over a campfire.

I drove north from my home in Lansing, crossing into the Upper Peninsula around 5 p.m. I drove west 16 miles to a national forest campground looking south over Lake Michigan. Before challenging myself with tent setup, I walked down to the water's edge. As is often the case over the Great Lakes, the sky seemed magnified in height and intensity of color. Puffy fair-weather clouds, like illustrations in the children's books I'd once read, were scattered across the heavens. Their white reflections were like swans silently gliding across the water.

I selected my campsite and turned to the business at hand. Although it took me over 20 minutes, I felt triumphant as I completed the task of erecting the tent. It was inviting, cozy. I would sleep well within its protective walls.

During the night, a surprise thunderstorm interrupted my sleep. It was not a dangerous storm. The few claps of thunder were tentative, like a nervous public speaker clearing his throat. The rain fell gently, like prayers, for a while. Then it came harder. Then, for about five minutes, the storm peaked, raindrops hurling themselves against the tent like medieval soldiers trying to bust down the walls of a fortress. That's when I felt the water ponding under the tarp below my sleeping bag. Soon, it began to wash between the tarp and the sleeping bag. My back started to dampen. But the rain ceased, and the campground fell silent. I fell asleep wet.

I awoke wetter. Aided by my imperfect tent positioning and assembly, the rain had penetrated most of the tent. Small circles of accumulated water filled all the indentations in the tarp. The bottom of the sleeping bag was soaked. There was nothing to do but laugh at myself.

Light was just beginning to dissolve the night, and my fellow campers weren't yet stirring. I crawled out of the tent and walked the few yards to my car, opened the trunk, and pulled out a towel and clothes to replace my overnight t-shirt and shorts over briefs. I also carried a bar of soap. Stealthily rounding a bend in the shoreline, I stopped at the lake's bath mat.

I slipped off my nightwear and slid into the cool Lake Michigan waters, shuddering for a moment. The lake slowly washed me clean. It wasn't merely a new day; it was a fresh start.

I thought of the vast extent of the lake and felt small, but reassuringly so. I was on vacation and was now seeing how puny my problems and anxieties were when measured against almost 1200 cubic miles of water.

Looking up, I saw an almost full moon high to the west. In the previous night's cloudiness, I had missed it. Now it was mute, still, peering down like an interested observer.

Like water flowing into my tent, a primal sensation rose up within me. I didn't understand it at first. I had no vocabulary for it. Finally, it translated itself into my language.

Men and women had come this way and camped here for hundreds, perhaps thousands of years, beholding the mystery of these large lakes. And at one indiscernible moment in the past, a man had done exactly as I was now doing in or close to this place. Crouching under a large moon in the corner of an unfathomably large body of water as day slowly took command, he had turned his eyes upward and wondered at the meaning of it all. But like me, only faster than me, he had understood without words, deeper than words. There was majesty in the moment.

Life itself made sense.

Chapter 4

Tony Infante was another person who knew more about the Great Lakes than most. He had for years doggedly, even courageously, at great cost to himself, pursued production of a video documentary on the Lakes. When I interviewed him, he was living in Bridgeport, not far from Saginaw, the city in which he'd been born.

Tony had spent more than 20 years in the golf world as a pro, a manufacturers' representative, a facility manager and developer, among other things. He had also worked in the hospitality industry. But something deeper inspired him – the Great Lakes. He gave up years of his life and much of his material comfort to make the documentary happen. He put it all on the line for the Lakes.

Where did his commitment come from? As was true of most people I interviewed, it all began in childhood. His early Great Lakes memories were family vacations on the Lake Huron shore. He remembered being "full of wonder and an eagerness to return to the shore that has never diminished."

He added, "My family always went on these trips with another family. We would rent small cottages on the shore at a place in Caseville that still exists, the Bella Vista. Six kids under the age of 6, the parents and a babysitter. I clearly remember swimming, flying kites and a lot of beach play. My family still has the Kodachrome slides of some of these trips. There were also two cottages on Lake Huron in Tawas, where a slide was actually in the lake several feet from the beach."

The trips ended after July 1970 when Tony's father perished in a car accident. In later years the family visited the Straits of Mackinac somewhat frequently, especially when family visited from New York and Italy. He remembered his Italian relatives, some of whom came from the small, seaside ancient village of Pisciotta, thinking "the beaches near Brevort in the U.P. were the most beautiful place they saw in the States, which makes profound sense to me now."

The recent Great Lakes memory that first came to mind was starkly different. He spent the better part of a day as an observer of an oil spill exercise in the Straits of Mackinac, a guest of Enbridge, the company that owned and operated an oil and gas pipeline that crossed the Straits deep beneath the water's surface. Not even the government regulators involved completely trusted Enbridge, which had been culpable in the largest inland oil spill in American history – in Michigan's Kalamazoo River watershed in 2010.

Tony was a regular user of the Lakes. "I love to swim in Lake Huron – it's a 30-minute drive from where I live, or Lake Michigan, it's 2.5-

hour drive," he said. "I have friends who invite me to sail in Lake St. Clair, the Straits of Mackinac and the Les Cheneaux Islands several times each year. There also hasn't been a day in thirty years where I don't think of the waters surrounding Mackinac Island. I lived and worked there for six summers, starting in 1986. I've returned frequently to visit and sometimes work ever since. He said he wasn't sure whether the Great Lakes were improving or slipping.

"I've come to believe the Lakes are endowed with powers of endurance and recuperation humans don't fully comprehend. On the other hand, it's clear that we as a so-called civilization continue to resist steps that would improve water quality."

Most of the people I interviewed chose Asian carp, toxic substances or something equivalent as the greatest menace to the Lakes. Tony cited "human ignorance, lack of curiosity in the ecosystem and the assumption that the Great Lakes will continue to provide the benefits that define our heritage and provide for our quality of life."

He said voting for candidates with knowledge and a record of advocacy on behalf of the Lakes was critical. The direct action he cited was purchasing environmentally sound products.

I wasn't surprised when Tony said he was both optimistic and pessimistic about the Great Lakes. Like others, he said he *needed* to be optimistic – in his case about the places he loved. "For the same reasons I care about my family and friends – they're the basis for my quality of life and gratitude. But I feel the future of the Great Lakes is endangered by our culture's willingness to use and monetize all natural resources without concern for sustainability or recognition of the complex interdependence of ecosystems."

He reverted to optimism when thinking about "the many different people and groups working on many different issues whether it's habitat restoration, ecological research and investigations, watershed nonprofits, shipwreck hunters and the occasional journalist, scholar and historian."

But there could be an overabundance of actors, too – especially in government, which he dubbed "the 100 flags of the Great Lakes. They create a mind-numbing gridlock. The only predictable outcomes of their meetings are more meetings."

He was particularly frustrated by the slow pace of government efforts to stop Asian carp from moving upstream in the Illinois River system through the Chicago Sanitary and Ship Canal into the Great Lakes. Too many cooks in the kitchen, he said. Government agencies had sparred over the use of electric barriers, the chemical Rotenone and fishing the species close to extinction. "Fishing these predators is a more effective means of preventing them from getting into the lakes. It's an idea that was overlooked for too long," he said.

One accomplishment to salvage from Great Lakes politics, he said, was the Great Lakes Restoration Initiative, for which Congress had appropriated approximately $2 billion by then. "I have gratitude for all the positive impacts and investments brought about during the last decade that can be traced directly to the formation and efforts of the Healing Our Waters coalition," he said, referring to an effort begun by Michigan philanthropist Peter Wege in 2004. "We would be far worse off without a movement borne and focused on the establishment of the GLR funding and its supporters from both parties."

My wrap-up question was the same one I asked each interview subject. If people care so much about the Great Lakes, why are they in mostly fair or poor condition according to the government itself?

Tony said the fault lies in ourselves. "Well, we continue to avoid making the changes and investments required to restore the health of the Great Lakes. My cynical answer is that the Great Lakes continue to provide humans with enough benefits that we won't care until enough people understand how our abuse of the ecosystem impacts our health or rapacious consumption."

His words were a little harsh, but the message was getting stronger: what were *we*, not *they*, doing to the Lakes?

Interlude 4

It's not always true what they say about the memory patterns of aging people. It's almost a proverb that the elderly remember clearly what happened decades ago, but it's yesterday they're foggy about. I can only speak for myself, but approaching the age of 60, I remembered yesterday vividly. I remember only a few scenes from February 11, 1985, the day six governors, representatives of other governors and Canadian premiers signed the Great Lakes Charter in Milwaukee, Wisconsin.

I remember flying from Lansing, Michigan to Milwaukee in a state-owned plane with my boss, Governor James Blanchard. It was a snowy day and through the cloud deck we couldn't see Lake Michigan, on whose behalf the chief executives were signing the Charter. When we arrived at the Milwaukee hotel for the signing, the lake was in view, clogged with ice.

I remember standing in a large room, perhaps a hotel ballroom, as New York's governor, Mario Cuomo, entered at the head of a legion of aides, including state police. The summer before, he had attracted national acclaim for a powerful speech at the Democratic National Convention and was considered likely presidential timber for 1988. Interest, and maybe even a trace of awe, rippled across the room.

I remember hearing Governor Blanchard tell reporters that the Charter was a signal to the Sunbelt that the Great Lakes region stood united, and would resist the transfer of water to that growing but arid section of the U.S.

I remember Tony Earl, the governor of Wisconsin and chairman of the Council of Great Lakes Governors, proclaiming the signing an historic occasion.

I remember wanting Earl to be right and thinking that February 11, 1985 might one day be regarded as a turning point in the history of the Great Lakes. Or maybe it was a hope, not simply a thought.

Thirty-one years later, I lived beside one of the Great Lakes, technically Huron-Michigan, whose level was 11 inches higher than the long-term monthly average for February. No one has drained Lake Huron-Michigan, but it's not the work of the Charter, or of its successor, the Great Lakes-St. Lawrence River Basin Water Resources Compact. The abundance of water in the Great Lakes on this day had to do with heavy precipitation and reduced evaporation – partially because of near-record ice cover the previous two winters. It's also the result of increased water use efficiency and, perhaps, the decline in water-intensive manufacturing in the region.

No one from the Sunbelt has seriously proposed diverting Great Lakes water since the Charter was signed, but the physical difficulty and mammoth expense of pumping and piping it from Chicago, say, to Texas has been the true impediment. The only bids for Great Lakes water that have originated outside the basin emerged from communities in the Great Lakes states themselves. Waukesha, Wisconsin was now seeking (and has since received) approval to divert approximately 10 million gallons a day from Lake Michigan to serve as its drinking water supply, replacing radium-tainted groundwater. This was the first request of its kind under the Compact, which was approved by

Congress and the President in 2008.

Like the Charter signing in 1985, enactment of the Compact captured considerable news coverage. Top government officials proclaimed the Compact an ironclad protection for the Great Lakes. In both cases leaders were well aware of the public clamor to defend Great Lakes water from Sunbelt bandits, a simple issue anyone could understand. This was as close to a case of good guys vs. bad guys as comes along in politics, and the politicians hastened to align themselves with good.

They also knew that an infinitesimal proportion of the public would read the Charter or Compact or follow their implementation, despite the emotional charge that convulsed the Great Lakes community each time a whiff of interest in diverting the region's freshwater was scented. And the elected officials knew the full bill for implementation — for the crucial but unexciting job of monitoring water use, developing conservation programs, and reviewing proposed major water uses by in-state and in-province parties — would come due after they left office. Inheriting someone else's promises, future governors and premiers might choose not to keep them, especially if it cost money.

And there was always that other issue: Congress ratified the Compact, giving its permission to the Great Lakes states to prohibit most water diversions. Congress could repeal it at any time. No one was talking about that. The Charter and the Compact left things in better shape, but they guaranteed nothing without vigilance that the citizenry was ill-equipped to provide.

I'd like to think that on February 11, 1985 I was hopeful rather than certain that the Great Lakes Charter would decisively change history. But I do remember how idealistic I was about public policy in 1985, and how easily I swooned at the enactment of a law or the signing of a document. It turned out that was only the beginning, and both inside and outside of government, there was little reckoning with that.

One could fault the politicians or the public — or both.

Chapter 5

Janine Middlesworth lived on Michigan's Lake Erie shore, facing the sunrise. And sometimes facing the algae monster.

In the years leading up to our exchange, western Lake Erie had suffered its biggest algae bloom in history and, in 2014, a smaller but unfortunately well-located bloom containing cyanotoxins had caused a drinking water emergency for 400,000 people in northwest Ohio and far southeast Michigan. For several days the city of Toledo had advised the public not to drink its treated water because of the toxin, present in an algae bloom at the city's water intake out in the lake. Depending on the winds and temperatures, Janine sometimes saw ugly algae at the shoreline.

Now in her 60s, Janine had primarily been a stay-at-home mother but had also worked outside of the home in retail, taught exercise, sold title insurance and was an artist.

Her earliest memory of Lake Erie was from a family vacation at Linwood Park in Vermillion, Ohio. "My dad rented a boat and I remember the splash! It was a whole new experience compared to static swimming pools."

But she was more focused on the ever-changing present – the lake she had known since she and her husband bought the home in 1972.

"My Lake Erie changes every single day. Last weekend my grandkids and I enjoyed swimming in waves like a wild ocean and then the next day swimming in a lake like glass. Not a ripple. We boat and tube, water ski, sail with friends, make sand castles, fish off the docks, look for snakes, and search for beach glass and lucky stones," she said.

She offered a clear-eyed, factual, pragmatic and indisputable perspective on protecting the Great Lakes – the sort of outlook you get outside the circle of wonks, advocates and scientists.

"Clean lakes are vital to wildlife, industry, tourism, drinking water, to life itself. Literally, what on Earth would you have without clean water?"

She sounded an optimistic note, saying the lakes "have improved immensely since the early 1970's. The water is crystal clear at least 10 months out of the year." Her "front row seat to the water" afforded her a close-up of the change. In 1972 daily masses of dead fish, soap suds and garbage joined algae as unsightly pollutants fouling her aquatic front yard.

Something puzzled her about the return of algae in the last decade. Governments had moved swiftly to curb Lake Erie's algae problem in the 1960s and early 1970s. Why was the problem returning? What was different now? "I look at green energy. I look at politics. Is it about money?"

Janine laid the blame for the recent Erie decline at the doorstep of agriculture, namely the over-fertilization of crops and the enormous amounts of animal waste generated by factory farms, both sending polluted runoff into the lake's tributaries. Should the animal waste from these immense farms go into sewer systems? Probably. But she saw another problem, and it was something that had been sold to the public as an environmental incentive.

"I've read numerous articles linking the new, green energy industry, ethanol, with creating the algae in lakes around the globe. More fertilizer, to grow more super corn, to make ethanol, means more excess phosphorous, more run off into lakes and streams. Dear farmers, politicians, scientists, citizens, it's nothing personal. Basically, the problem seems to be chemical reactions. Why can't we have clean water and clean air?"

What could a citizen do? Talk about the issues with neighbors, family and friends, get involved in local 'save the water' groups, write letters to government officials, call radio and TV stations to share pictures, share them on social media, and "read, read, read."

Taking the long view, Janine expressed optimism about the future of the Great Lakes. "I've witnessed amazing change already in my lifetime. The absolute best thing that ever happened to draw attention to the algae problem in my area was the water crisis in Toledo. I was ecstatic! Finally, people will now wake up and pay attention to this algae issue. It's amazing to me that people don't associate these giant bodies of water with what comes out of their faucets."

Pollution of Lake Erie, she said, was both personal and political. Personal because she and neighbors lived with the lake every day, political because the solutions would require government action. "I think we run in to trouble when it gets down to money and special interests, PACs and lobbyists. The forward motion grinds to a halt. Too many cooks in the kitchen spoil the broth. Too many politicians pollute the lake."

But government wasn't alone in the fight. "To me, care means monitoring the lakes and at the same time leaving them alone! Don't bury junk, don't dump junk, don't build junk, don't sell the water! Why does it seem so simple?"

She wasn't parochial; her regard extended to all of the Great Lakes. "I love my Lake Erie and I love my home here and all the memories that we have created. But I know all the Great Lakes need care. All the water around the world needs care."

It was interesting to encounter someone who'd seen the lakes for more than four decades and was optimistic. I wondered whether younger people or those farther from the Lakes would be hopeful, too.

Interlude 5

Perhaps part – but not all – of the gap between our love of the lakes and their deteriorating condition has to do with the modern orientation of government. While it is too easy to lay blame for the suffering Lakes exclusively at the feet of federal, state, provincial and municipal officials, certain instances reveal public servants more committed to their mandates or to the industry lobby groups that court them than to their constituents. The drinking water catastrophe in Flint, Michigan is only the most spectacular example.

As western Lake Erie slid into disgraceful condition in 2011, Ohio lawmakers and appointed officials there and in Michigan initially resisted meaningful actions to address the runoff pollution feeding harmful algal blooms in the lake. Their reluctance wasn't difficult to explain. As the leading source of the runoff, agriculture needed to curb its commercial phosphorus fertilizer and phosphorus-rich animal waste application. Always a powerful political lobby, agriculture traditionally – and in this case at first -- resisted enforceable restrictions on its phosphorus use.

In 2014, Michigan's Department of Environmental Quality, for example, sent letters to agricultural facility operators with concentrated animal feeding operations in the state's portion of the Lake Erie Basin more or less pleading with them, pretty please, to refrain from applying waste in the winter. If they intended to apply the state asked for the courtesy of a 48-hour notice. "Notifying the DEQ prior to winter application and/or manifesting is not a permit requirement at this time and failure to do so is not a permit violation," the DEQ said. "However, we ask for your voluntary cooperation to demonstrate Michigan CAFOs' stewardship and dedication to Michigan's water quality."

Such begging for cooperation, when the lake was in critical condition, deeply offended some citizen watchdogs. But the contamination of Toledo's public drinking water supply in August 2014 shook things loose politically – in Ohio. With relative speed, the Ohio State Legislature enacted a law banning the application of animal waste and commercial fertilizer on frozen, snow-covered or saturated ground. Hoping to avoid the tarnishing of its reputation through intransigence, the Ohio Farm Bureau negotiated and then supported the legislation. The new law had several faults – limiting itself only to the western Lake Erie Basin, providing exceptions, and largely depending on scarce citizen complaints for enforcement – but it was responsive to the crisis and to public concerns. Michigan, meanwhile, sent out the imploring letters.

In 2015, Michigan put together a strategy to reduce phosphorus runoff from its waters flowing into Lake Erie by 40%. It barely mentioned agriculture. "That's straight out of the Big Ag and Conservation District/NRCS propaganda handbook," said advocate Pam Taylor. "Same old, same old - it's not ag in general, and anyway even if it was, Michigan doesn't have any livestock in that area, which has changed to yes, Michigan does have livestock in that watershed but they're so few that they can't be contributing anything."

In another instance, Ohio joined Michigan in intransigence. Frustrated with the slide of Lake Erie water quality, environmental groups called on the two states to place the algae-choked open waters of the lake's western basin on an "impaired waters" list under the U.S. Clean Water Act. Listing would launch a process in which U.S. EPA would determine the maximum amount of phosphorus pollution the basin could accept without unacceptable algae blooms. Then EPA and the two states (three, if Indiana's share of the Maumee River were included) would identify sources of the phosphorus causing the algae outbreaks, allocate reduction targets for the sources – including agriculture – and set goals and timelines for reduction to assure accountability. Although requiring years to implement, a comparable process was beginning to show results in the Chesapeake Bay. It had the potential to reform agricultural practices.

Ohio and Michigan governments rejected the impaired waters listing for eyebrow-raising reasons. A representative of Ohio Governor and 2016 presidential hopeful John Kasich declared that listing the western Lake as impaired would degrade the lake's national reputation and branding efforts. "It is a tag that is going to go on Lake Erie," said Karl Gephardt of Ohio EPA. "The message would be this: Lake Erie is impaired." According to these officials, the international publicity that the Toledo drinking water contamination crisis attracted in 2014 apparently had not harmed the Lake's image.

Michigan had a simpler answer. Bradley Wurfel, the Michigan Department of Environmental Quality's spokesperson – who would later resign as part of the bloodletting after the Flint disaster – told a reporter, "There is no way the state would take that action yet...One, there are no support studies completed that would buttress that determination. Two, Michigan has already done a ton to reduce phosphorus inputs to the lake, and we're doing more all the time."

It was a case of what to believe, a state official or one's lying eyes examining the unsightly, even repugnant waters of western Lake Erie in the late summer. Even the existence of alarming science did not impress Wurfel. Finally, in late 2016, Michigan did list its share of the open waters of Lake Erie as impaired, and in 2018 – pressured by the courts – Ohio did the same -- but by then a new administration in Washington was in power and would have no interest in federal oversight of state water pollution efforts.

One approach to curing the lake's agriculture-promoted algal blooms that politicians hastened to act on was the doling out of taxpayer funding to farmers in support of agriculture best management practices to reduce phosphorus runoff voluntarily. Offending no farmer or lobbyist and pleasing the subsidy recipients, new money poured onto Lake Erie watershed farms after enactment in 2014 of a U.S. farm bill. The legislation created a Regional Conservation Partnership Program, or RCPP, to stimulate the creation of nonfederal collaborative processes testing and implementing emerging practices with the potential to reduce phosphorus runoff. In its first year in law, the program dished out $17.3 million for a western basin Lake Erie collaborative. Well-

intentioned, it promised to repeat the results of the previous 30 years of federal funding of agriculture's voluntary environmental work – gradually unraveling lakes.

The circle that put together the partnership, and resisted regulation of agriculture, was insular, forming a barrier that outside interested parties could not penetrate.

Chapter 6

Melissa Molenda was a force of nature even before she went to work in communications for The Nature Conservancy. She attacks work and celebrates life with gusto and her laugh injects a feel-good humor virus into anyone who hears it. In addition, she has finely developed instincts for communicating with mass audiences. I had known her for 20 years but never asked about her thoughts or feelings about the Great Lakes.

Born in LaGrange, Illinois, Melissa had spent most of her life in, and was a resident of the Lansing area when I interviewed her. That's about as far from a Great Lake as you can get in Michigan. She was in her mid-40s with a teenaged daughter.

"The earliest I can remember experiencing the Great Lakes was going with my friend's grandparents on their yacht around Mackinac Island," Melissa said. "I remember feeling very excited and happy yet small and overwhelmed. The best thing I remember is the smell. I brought my favorite baby blanket with me and remember smelling it for weeks afterwards, trying to get a whiff of the watery air."

Not long before the interview, she had traveled with a Conservancy work team for a hike of the dunes at Saugatuck, on Lake Michigan. She called the view spectacular. "Truly breathtaking. Those dunes make me very proud of my home state."

Much of Melissa's contact with the Great Lakes was indirect and through her job. "I see the lakes every day in photography, whether it's on social media like Instagram or in viewing photographers' galleries. I don't see them very often in person since I live two hours away from the nearest one. I'm not a beach person and don't naturally think of going to the lakes when considering a day trip."

When I asked her how important it was to protect the Great Lakes, she took an interesting turn, focusing on the "protect" instead of "important."

"The word 'protect' is always a weird one to me for environmental advocacy. In essence, we need to 'protect' the lakes from ourselves and the damage that ill-informed people do. Sometimes we've damaged the lakes without knowing it or find out later about some effect from a practice started decades ago. Nature will always adapt and the planet will be fine, but the water may be toxic to humans and wildlife if we don't take care of it, respect and treat it with care."

Never a pessimist, Melissa saw no reason for despair in the Lakes' current problems. "It's an up and down cycle, sometimes because of not knowing harmful effects until later, from pollution to invasive species. We damage it, find out about it, correct and restore mistakes, and then something else happens again to start the cycle all over. If we evolve and do better, the lakes will be cleaner and healthier."

The top threat to the health of the Great Lakes was not out there, it was in us, she said.

"The biggest problem is people and ignorance, or perhaps more specifically, out of sight, out of mind. It's hard to see how excessive fertilizer 90 miles away from a Great Lake will have an effect. I've seen an old refrigerator dumped on the side of a river and I'm floored by the selfishness of people not caring about their individual actions."

The sun came out when she looked ahead. "I'm more optimistic than ever before because I've seen an awakening in the products sold in stores, the way people think and buy and a general awareness about our connection between people and nature whether it's the weather and climate change or invasive species and globalization. We have a lot more choices and a lot more understanding about compatibility and sustainable solutions."

Melissa had a wide social circle, so I was curious what her friends said about the Great Lakes. If the subject came up, she said, it was purely in a personal situation when talking about going to a beachside town or taking a vacation. "People in my personal circle don't talk about political issues involving the lakes and they're generally unaware. When you fly over Lake Michigan, it looks fine."

Did she have a favorite Great Lake? "I feel more connected or stronger about Lake Michigan than any other lake. It's more culturally significant and actually seems the most beautiful. Lake Superior is amazing and extraordinary, but also cold and remote. Lake Huron seems dirty and gross, and Lake Erie seems like Ohio. I've never seen Lake Ontario and don't really care about it." I forgot to mention she's brutally honest.

Plugged into pop culture as she is, Melissa was the woman to ask about Great Lakes art, books or movies. "I can't recall any movies specifically about the Great Lakes, only used in the background like when Tom Cruise lost his dad's car in Lake Michigan in *Risky Business*."

I thanked her and mused on her journey from office work to lead for The Conservancy's Great Lakes communications. She was right for the job. She knew all the reasons why the Lakes were in trouble, but she remained optimistic in spite of them.

Interlude 6

My career has given me abundant opportunities to work with Canadians, primarily through two institutions that deal with the resources of the Great Lakes. As an appointee to the Great Lakes Fishery Commission, I participated in meetings and decisions associated with invasive sea lamprey control and management of the fishery among the various jurisdictions on both sides of the border. As a staff member of the International Joint Commission, I served appointees who offered advice to the Canadian and U.S. governments on issues covered by the umbrella of the Great Lakes Water Quality Agreement. Both institutions operated on the principles of parity and consensus. Although the population of the U.S. is more than 10 times that of Canada, the nations have equal representation on each commission. And rare is the decision achieved by divided vote — or vote at all, rather than collective assent.

I can attest that at the levels of both commissioner and staff, parity is generally twinned with collegiality in the everyday operations of the commissions. What does that really mean?

First, Canadians and Americans share more than a common tongue (although French in Quebec and Spanish across the U.S. are also robust, and First Nations and tribes maintain their traditional languages). We share values, one of which is the importance of conserving natural resources.

Second, Canadians and Americans respect each other. Peace has prevailed between what are now two sovereign nations for two centuries. The two commissions I've served are part of a broader set of instruments the two nations use to prevent and resolve disputes and maintain cordiality, not just peace. These mechanisms articulate the implicit direction of two peoples to cooperate in the mutual interest.

Third, Canadians and Americans equally appreciate the Great Lakes. The imaginary international boundary that traverses four of them means less than the majesty that spans them. Cooperation is critical in the protection of shared waters.

As an American, I've noted several characteristics of my Canadian colleagues and their countrymen and women. These are generalizations, of course, with many human exceptions.

Canadians are, by and large, fundamentally more civil than brash Americans. In commission business, they are less prone to erupt in anger or hostility and more likely to maintain calm and reason in tense situations involving the two nations' delegations. That does not mean they are less emotional than Americans — only that they tend to control themselves.

They have a patience for process that Americans lack. In fact, they sometimes seem to have a process fetish, while Americans exalt the value of speedy (or hasty) decisions.

They are modest about their nation's achievements and skeptical in a healthy way about grand pronouncements, which American politicians and public servants tend to offer. Their national self-effacement contrasts sharply with American braggadocio.

What Americans aren't generally engaged in is an effort to understand Canadian history, or even Canadian perspectives on events involving both nations. How many in the U.S. recognize that some Canadians think of the War of 1812 as a repelling of a U.S. invasion and a successful stand for territorial integrity?

Similarly, the Canadians I've known tend to be more aware of events in the U.S. than Americans are of events in Canada. A U.S. visitor to Canada turns on the television in her hotel room to find a third or more of the programming American. Imagine the tables turned, and both English and French-language Canadian programming everywhere on U.S. televisions. Americans might learn something about our friendly neighbors.

A few differences in parlance can be initially jarring. For example, when a Canadian government tables a proposal, it is offering the idea for consideration. When an American government tables a proposal, it is withdrawing it from consideration. I'd never heard of a secondment until I joined the Fishery Commission or a casual hire until I joined the International Joint Commission.

In Great Lakes governance, Canadians do not always have equal footing with Americans. The Great Lakes Commission, established by interstate compact approved by Congress in 1968, in conception included Canadian members, but Congress did not assent to this portion of the Compact, in defense of federal government prerogatives to conduct foreign policy. Instead, Ontario and Quebec representatives participate in Commission meetings as observers. Similarly, representatives of the two provinces participate without formal voting powers in review, deliberation and decision-making regarding new or increased water diversions under the 2008 Great Lakes-St. Lawrence Basin Sustainable Water Resources Compact. In the latter case, it is also true that the U.S. states cannot vote on new or increased water diversions in Ontario but do participate as observers under an agreement among the jurisdictions.

Despite these legal limitations, there is truly no boundary between the two nations and their civil servants in strength of sentiment and allegiance regarding the Great Lakes. Both communities recognize the singularity of the Lakes and both prize them. Both, in the end, will subordinate their differences in the interest of protecting the Lakes from harm.

As my career and I aged, my definition of Canadian evolved as much as my definition of American has. I worked with aboriginals, an Indian-Canadian, and an African-Canadian. Similarly, my understanding of the Canadian character – to the extent one can be said to exist – has evolved. The stereotype of the over-apologetic, humble to meek and unexcitable Canadian temperament contains shards of truth but is also a vast oversimplification. Canadians are as varied in character as any people. But they are as devoted as they are essential in common work on our shared treasure, the Great Lakes.

Chapter 7

Catherine Masson is an intellectual, and a swimmer. She's warm as well as analytical, and easy to interview as thoughts pour out in precise, often elegant words, spoken or written.

Fifty-something when I interviewed her, Catherine was born in London, Ontario. She characterized her earliest reaction to the Great Lakes as "Awe, and shock that something this big existed in our world and no one told me about it."

Her early Great Lakes memories featured fish. "For 25 years, our family kept a 24-foot fishing boat at Port Credit marina, near Mississauga. We fished for (stocked) Pacific salmon and Lake Trout. My Dad did very well in the yearly Toronto Star Salmon Derby, often placing near the top. He had all the gear, rods, reels, downriggers, sonar, CB radio and 19 tackle boxes."

But the resulting feasts were denied the children. Contaminants in Great Lakes fish prompted health authorities to issue fish consumption advisories. The warnings "were widely shared and with the age-appropriate explanations, elders told children we would not be partaking in the feast. Adults enjoyed the abundant, oversize catch steamed, broiled, barbequed, fried, smoked and pickled, while we looked on in wonder."

Summers in her youth also brought relaxed days at Grand Bend on Lake Huron, Thunder Beach in Georgian Bay, Port Dover on Lake Erie. The family enjoyed weekend parties at friends' beachfront homes, Catherine said. "Swimming at waterfront cottages on lakes large and small became synonymous with coming-of-age."

Swimming was a theme spanning Catherine's past and present. She had enjoyed swimming all five of the Great Lakes and the St. Lawrence River; in the summer of 2017 alone she swam Lakes Ontario, Huron and Superior.

"Great Lakes open water swimming is my new personal challenge," she reported. In the summer of 2016 she volunteered for the Lake Ontario Waterkeeper at the Toronto Island Lake Swim and at the last minute, chose to swim the 1.5 K in a borrowed suit. "Not as elegant or tactical as the high-performance swimmers and triathletes, but I prevailed through a foot of chop along the beach to the finish. Lake Ontario looks so familiar and feels so different when you're in it," she said.

In 2017, she signed up for the Lake Ontario Swim Team (LOST), open water swimmers and triathletes meeting weekly at the Lighthouse Pier in historic downtown Oakville. She resolved to swim the 2017 LOST Mile (1.6 km). Picking up her play-by-play:

"Thunderstorms rolled through the day before the race, dropping surface temperatures from a comfortable 68°F/20°C to a chilly 50°F/10°C. For safety, the LOST mile is cut to 500-metres and the 3.8 K becomes a 750-metre race. Due to insurance regulations, wetsuits are mandatory and organizers put an ad hoc buddy system in place for last minute gear sharing. First time ever in a neoprene wetsuit – yet another open water adaptation. We line up for the in-water start. Horn blows and we're off! It's hard to see other swimmers through the dense surface fog, easier to spot underwater bodies through the green gloom. I catch the rhythm and sight direction to stay straight, rolling with waves, exhaling underwater, saving leg power for the sprint-to-finish. Challenging to reach the rocky shore, get vertical fast and run for the big inverted U finish line – without slipping or toppling over. The computer chip around my ankle certifies my time. Eighth woman overall. I did it!"

It sounded as though Catherine had undergone an aquatic metamorphosis. "I will swim anywhere so long as conditions are safe. I am only truly at home, happy and comfortable when enfolded by water. At such times, there is the sensation that water and I are one being without end, beyond membranes, barriers or boundaries. I seek to be resilient like water and take the path of least resistance."

I knew she would have thought-provoking things to say in response to my question about the gap between public love for the lakes and their mediocre condition.

"How do we understand the diversity of Great Lakes ecosystems when our own drinking water arrives via plumbing and plastic bottles, and disappears down drains, toilets and gutters? When large populations experience potable water supplied in this manner, they are less engaged with the living, running freshwaters. Water has suffered abuses of displacement and disruption that mirrors our dissociation from it."

She offered a second explanation that I heard from no one else: shifting social baselines. These are "an underestimated challenge for long-term freshwater protection and restoration. The baselines of great-grandparents, grandparents, parents, brothers and sisters, children, grandchildren and great-grandchildren are all different and shift over time. Our personal reference states are established in childhood and youth, and tend to become fixed through one's lifetime. New arrivals do not automatically have the same convictions and interest, nor the same understanding of 'place.' Public awareness work is never done. It's a problem of dynamic memory loss – people relocate, move on to other jobs or retire. It's very difficult to change this psychology, so the phenomenon needs recognition as an insidious force contributing to the acceptance of current conditions as the norm.

The new norm was that degraded and non-sustainable conditions tend to be accepted as management targets. Ecologists and managers, victims of the phenomenon, often accept that environmental conditions of the immediate past reflect conditions in the intermediate and distant past, she observed.

But Catherine had a thought on how to reclaim the watershed's destiny. During my time at the International Joint Commission, she had collected and analyzed what was surely the largest body ever of Great Lakes vision statements by governments, nonprofits, businesses and associations, in the hope of convincing IJC to articulate and build consensus on a shared vision to reawaken latent energy.

"Vision statements are integral to 21st century strategic planning," she wrote me. "In bold language, visions and principles describe preferred futures – and why they matter. As Great Lakes and St. Lawrence River basin governance evolves, the challenges of building a shared vision for regional renewal and long-term transformation remain unsolved. Despite dedicated appeals and determined efforts, our region is still without this vital change instrument."

I wasn't sure even a vision statement agreed upon by all the many Great Lakes managers would result in dramatic change. But it couldn't hurt. Maybe the other 34,999,000 of us in the watershed should sign on too.

Interlude 7

A U.S. EPA official from Washington, D.C. headquarters traveled to the agency's regional office in Chicago for a daylong meeting. As the noon hour arrived, he mentioned that he liked to jog instead of taking lunch and would run along Lake Michigan. "Do you think I can circle the lake and be back when we start up again at one?"

Probably intended by the EPA regional staff to mock out-of-touch Washington, the apocryphal tale does contain a trace of truth. The vastness of the Great Lakes is news to some from outside the region. Conversely, the vulnerability of the Lakes is often a surprise to local policymakers and the public alike.

Hubris and false humility are co-inhabitants of environmental country today. On the one hand, faith abounds in humankind's technological power. If we can make smart phones, surely we can vanquish pollution. Yet at the same time we offer up this faith in our species' transcendent smarts, we deny our capacity to degrade an ecosystem as large as the Great Lakes.

The notion that human communities simply can't have profound impact on natural resources is nothing new in the region. Lumber interests in the mid-1800s scoffed at the suggestion that their operations could have ruinous impact on the forests of the upper Great Lakes states. Timber was for all practical purposes inexhaustible, they said, and would last 500 years. It lasted a little more than 50 and lumbering left in its wake a landscape of hideous ruin. It took another 50 years and hundreds of millions of dollars of tax revenues to regrow the forests so they could be sustainably managed – much of it in the public domain.

Faced with almost one-fifth of the world's freshwater, residents of the Great Lakes watershed have failed to understand the potential effect of human beings on such a massive treasure. The Great Lakes are so big they'll dilute our pollution until it's harmless, our ancestors said in the late 1800s. By the early 20th Century, the Lakes were a polluted disgrace.

Today, consciousness of the Great Lakes' vulnerability to threats is mixed. The most publicized and sensational looming dangers leaping behemoth Asian carp and toxic substances – command respect. They emerge from outside; in fact, Asian carp and their ilk are commonly referred to as alien species with all the pejoratives that term connotes.

But these vast lakes are also vulnerable to threats from within. Luxury housing is encroaching on sensitive coastal wetlands, killing off biological diversity in those habitats little by little. Open space in urban and suburban areas is being consumed by roads and buildings, driving up pollution of Great Lakes tributaries and the Lakes themselves by conveying fouled water directly to them rather than capitalizing on the filtering properties of soils and vegetation. Individually, housing projects and paved roads have limited effect, but cumulatively across the basin, they deeply degrade the system. Yet it is difficult for many to comprehend or care about these threats, or to believe they imperil the Great

Lakes.

It may be time to popularize the Great Lakes as the Greatly Fragile Lakes. They are robust enough to recover when we cease our destructive actions, but the likelihood that we will do so is less if we think of them as the Greatly Indestructible Lakes.

Chapter 8

Facebook can be a marvelous thing. When I put out the word that I wanted to interview people about the Great Lakes, Betsy Alles replied.

Although she had been born and spent much of her life in Michigan, I barely knew her. When she answered my questions, I wished I did.

Betsy had enjoyed a career spanning corporate communication for large companies, ownership of her own marketing agency for a decade, fund development for a nonprofit environmental group, and serving as CEO of the Michigan YMCA. She was now executive director of the Sheboygan County, Wisconsin, Chamber of Commerce. She said she watched "the changing moods of Lake Michigan from all the windows in my house in Manitowoc."

The same lake assisted her work, she said. "We are so fortunate to have this amazing resource at our doorstep, and it's become my theme in ten years of leadership of two chambers of commerce here. What used to look like a limitation to land commerce is now viewed as our number one asset."

Federal involvement in the Great Lakes region wasn't always viewed favorably, but Betsy was in hot pursuit of a national marine sanctuary designation for waters of Lake Michigan offshore from Sheboygan County. Modeled after the Thunder Bay Marine Sanctuary off Alpena, Michigan, the Wisconsin version would preserve and commemorate shipwrecks. She forecast "a tremendous impact on education, preservation and business in our region."

It was fitting that Betsy was capping her career by the shores of Lake Michigan, which "has had a magnetic effect on me from the time I got my driver's license in Battle Creek. Every weekend possible we would load up our car and head for the lake. I always swore I would live within sight of her and now have had that privilege in five different places since 2002."

"But I also have very deep feelings for Lake Superior. Every summer we bike the Keweenaw Peninsula and fly to the Apostle Islands."

Across the lake from Sheboygan County was Betsy's favorite Great Lakes scenery, from Point Betsie Lighthouse north to Sleeping Bear Dunes. "Every fall we rent one of the places at Point Betsie for a week," she said. "The setting, lighting and views are spectacular. That's our family gathering spot. When we lived in Empire our favorite thing to do was to run down the dune on Pierce Stocking Drive and walk the beach to Empire. It was the swimming and body surfing along the way that I loved the most. And, of course, falling asleep on the beach."

She reinforced a message that I was receiving consistently – that even people personally or professionally engaged in Great Lakes policy did not hear much about those issues outside of work hours. "It's is always the love of the lakes that makes these issues so important. In Wisconsin we talk a lot about how the lake used to be the center of manufacturing and how some people still stay away from it because of that. But mostly over here, people talk about the potential posed by the marine sanctuary."

I'd asked almost everyone I interviewed whether they'd enjoyed anything about the Great Lakes in the arts. Most couldn't think of any arts involving the Lakes. Betsy could. She'd watched "Step Into Liquid," a video that highlights the freshwater surfing in Sheboygan. I had never heard of Great Lakes surfing until a few years before – now it was nationally recognized.

Despite her sunny attitude toward the marine sanctuary proposal, Betsy assessed the Lakes as worsening. She could see algae blooms and zebra mussel shells out her window. She lived across the street from one of the largest factory farms in Wisconsin. As a result, no doubt, she put agricultural "and other" runoff at the top of her list of threats to the Lakes.

"Agriculture has a very strong influence in Wisconsin. How do we partner with agriculture to identify, support, promote and advocate for alternative ways to manage the manure issue?" She was astonished how much manure a factory farm produced with relatively little pollution control when balanced with the rigorous requirements applying to her household septic system.

As for individual action to protect the Lakes, that would have to take a back seat. "In Wisconsin, we first have to begin to educate people in a meaningful way – children and adults – about the value and the fragility of the Great Lakes. At the same time, we have to advocate for fines that are large enough to discourage these major corporate CAFOs (concentrated animal feeding operations) from practices that might result in 'accidental' leakage. Then we need to talk about limits on bovine populations in certain areas. When I heard that we will now export more and more beef and milk products I realized that these farms will grow even larger. I could go on and on."

But, she added, "I'm always hopeful and perhaps it's because I am allowed and encouraged to express my optimism and my love of the Great Lakes in my position as an economic development advocate. I believe balance is always possible, people value healthy choices and they just need to have their eyes opened."

Why were the lakes deteriorating when so many people care about them? "'Many' is not enough," Betsy said. "People are busy, don't listen and make poor choices when they're not presented information in the way they learn best. A crowd does not constitute a majority."

By the time I checked back with her before publishing this book, the tides had turned against the Lake Michigan marine sanctuary. Wisconsin

Governor Scott Walker withdrew his support, siding with some lakefront property owners who feared federal incursion on their rights. Betsy penned a response to her area newspaper.

"I am a lakefront property owner," she wrote. "It's a privilege I will never take for granted. As such, I am also very much aware of my responsibilities as a citizen and a human-being on this planet to bring the greatest amount of appreciation and protection to this amazing body of fresh water. We are all the keepers of Her majesty and Her riches. According to some economic research, She and her Sisters will be the reason our regional economy will survive and even thrive in the coming decades."

Because of the sanctuary, she said, "More people will venture out on the water to explore. Our kids and grandkids will have access to a vast scientific and historical playground. New businesses will develop to provide services to visitors and those who live here."

The political setback did not diminish her determination. She said she might take up environmental education concerning the Lakes. Betsy's soul was, quite clearly, attached to Lake Michigan. "Its waves and her drama," she said, "are part of me as much as the beating of my heart or my breath going in and out."

And what one word would she apply to the Lakes? Fresh.

Interlude 8

Sometimes, when the public does articulate its feelings unequivocally on a Great Lakes issue, its expressed desire mobilizes government to act – and frustrate the public will. If citizens find out, their cynicism is heightened, but a public relations offensive can overwhelm any possibility of discovery.

In 1998, a Canadian company, the Nova Group, quietly obtained a permit from the province of Ontario to transport over 150 million gallons per year of Lake Superior water by vessel for sale to customers in Asia. Word got out. A storm of public outrage ensued. John Febrraro, the Nova Group head, complained in May 1998 that after news of his permit broke, "I've not had a moment's peace. I've been fielding telephone calls from across North America."

The idea of selling Great Lakes waters for private profit sickened the populace. Taking note, the company surrendered the permit, and government officials began discussions on new restrictions on the transfer of water out of the Great Lakes watershed.

Restrictions already existed, but they covered pipelines and canals, not vessels as water conveyances. Both the 1985 Great Lakes Charter and Section 1109 of the federal Water Resources Development Act of 1986 – which required approval by all eight Great Lakes State governors of new or increased diversions – had nothing to say about export.

The process of strengthening controls on diversions and exports spanned a decade. Governors and premiers, government agency officials, environmental advocates, business lobbyists and attorneys researched and negotiated new protections. In 2005 they gave to the world a proposed interstate compact (and corresponding, good-faith agreement among the Great Lakes states, Ontario and Quebec) to prohibit almost all diversions. In effect, the binding Compact would take the place of the non-binding Charter. Three years later, after remarkable word-for-word concurrence by the 16 chambers of the legislatures of the Great Lakes states and their governors and approval by Congress, President George W. Bush signed the Compact into law.

The heralded Compact had been born out of fierce public opposition to the sale of Great Lakes water. Therefore, the Compact banned the sale of Great Lakes water, correct? No. In fact, the Compact explicitly exempted from the diversion prohibition the transport of water in containers of 5.7 gallons or less in volume. It also exempted from the diversion prohibition water used in the basin to "manufacture or produce a Product that is then transferred out of the Basin or watershed."

It did, however, ban the transfer of Great Lakes water out of the basin in tanker ships in bulk; therefore, the specter of a navy of freighters floating from Lake Superior to Asia dematerialized. But if each vessel in the navy held Lake Superior water in plastic 2-liter bottles for sale, and the navy was as big as the U.S. fleet, the Compact would not interfere.

How could a clear public consensus that spurred the negotiation of the Compact be disregarded in the final document that became state and federal law? There are two commonly offered explanations and a third that is, more powerful. First, opponents of a ban on sale of Great Lakes water in containers said the impact of bottling and selling the liquid would be negligible. Nestle Corporation's controversial water pumping and bottling operation in Mecosta County, Michigan affected local streams but the impact on Lake Michigan was imperceptible.

Second, proponents of the exemptions said water should be treated as a product like water-based substances. Doug Roberts Jr., director of environmental and energy policy at the Michigan Chamber of Commerce, called it "critical that you are able to make products and ship them all over the world. That's what you do in a free-market economy. We were very concerned groups would target one product and say that product can't be shipped. What's the difference between bottled water and beer or cherry juice? Those all have water in them." The difference, of course, was that water was water, and beer had water in it. Another difference was that you can live without beer but not without water.

The most powerful reason for the language carving out the special treatment for the sale of water in small containers was that the water-for-sale industry's representatives had inside access to the negotiating table. Their friendly relations with government negotiators served them well. But they conducted themselves amicably as well with the public interest representatives on the staff of environmental organizations. In the end, regardless of whatever reservations they may have had about the sale of Great Lakes water, environmentalists agreed to the deal, thinking it on balance a good bargain.

Approval of the Compact by the U.S. Congress was not unanimous. The U.S. House of Representatives supported it 390 to 25. Most of the 25 "no" voters objected to the water sale loophole. One of them, Congressman Bart Stupak of Michigan, challenged the Compact's implicit approval of selling Great Lakes water, saying that once state and federal law sanctioned it, free trade agreements would open the door to sale to any entrepreneur. That, in turn, would risk both domestic control of the lakes. In 2009, Stupak introduced a resolution that would have expressed the sense of Congress that "the definition of diversion ... and the exception for 'products' from such definition, did not intend that water itself in any size container or package is a 'product' and exempt from the definition of diversion subject to the compact." The resolution died.

This was a case where the public unambiguously expressed a preference on a Great Lakes environmental issue, and ten years of labor by a legion of political insiders thwarted it. But very few members of the public knew this. They heard time and again from Compact proponents and reporters that the Compact fully protected the Great Lakes.

Chapter 9

Stephanie Prechter's path crossed mine in October 2017 when, after she lunched with a mutual friend, she sent me a short e-mail saying my name had come up.

"I am currently doing research for my take on the Great Lakes Project," she wrote. "As a photography student at Washtenaw Community College in Ann Arbor, MI, this has evolved into a passion project and something I am looking to expand on." She sent me a link to her Project. The most important word in my response, after viewing her work, was "wow." Her eye was exquisite.

The accompanying prose wasn't bad, either. "Growing up on an island in the Detroit River, I naturally developed a strong personal reverence and connection to the lakes," she wrote on her site. "I recall looking out on the river mesmerized by the freighters rolling by, zipping through the channel by boat, the risky lighthouse jumps into the swift current, and spending time immersed in fresh water.

"Photography opened up a new awareness for me serving as a porthole into a network of lighthouse keepers, the inner workings of our shipping industry, and the majesty of these lakes," she wrote.

Her work was of such quality that in February 2018 it merited a solo exhibition at a gallery in Maumee, Ohio, outside of Toledo.

Given Stephanie's background and poetic spirit, I wanted to interview her. Thirty-seven years old at the time we exchanged e-mails, she said Grosse Ile had been her childhood perch on the Detroit River. That placed her in the area generally described by the people of southeast Michigan as "Downriver Detroit." She now lived in Ann Arbor.

Her experience in the arts, she said on her website, "varies from mixed media to the darkroom, work in the studio, alternative processes, and most recently a collaborative internship with the University of Michigan Cancer Center offering photography as an outlet to patients and their families. I aspire to share the beauty of image with others and in essence offer a space for newfound appreciation."

She elaborated on her ties to the Great Lakes, ranging from early-in-life summer boating and lighthouse jumping to her recent photography of these great waters. I could see from her website gallery that she had traveled for this, with photos of the North Breakwater Light at Ludington and lighthouse keepers in Muskegon, among others. The photos underscored that her work wasn't just about beaches or freighters or lighthouses or water. She had stopped to interview those who felt about the Lakes as she did.

Pictured was Mike, who tended to the Fort Gratiot Lighthouse in Port

Huron. "This is the gateway to the western Great Lakes," he told her. "It is my home. Doing this work is a way for me to honor this land and the lakes."

Stephanie seemed to be doing her work for the same reason.

When I interviewed her, she had not yet completed the circuit of the Lakes, not yet having seen Lake Ontario. She resisted identifying a favorite spot among the Lakes but singled out the Detroit River for mention because of its familiarity. Stephanie made an effort to see one of the Lakes at least once a month.

She knew where her drinking water originated and her sewage flowed. As an Ann Arbor resident, she was served by a municipal drinking water system that took 85% of its volume from the Huron River, and 15% from groundwater. Ann Arbor's wastewater treatment plant handled the effluent.

She believed the Lakes were improving in some ways and declining in others. "I think some things are better in that we have research, education, and awareness; but at the same time, we're lacking in a deeper understanding as to how much of an impact our actions can have on the lakes," she told me. "I know the invasive species including the algae blooms and the quagga mussels have a huge impact, as do the industry that surrounds the lakes. They say that the clarity of the lakes is not an indicator of a healthy lake, it's the indicator of a lake being sucked of its nutrients."

Her one-word answer when asked to identify the number one threat to the health of the Great Lakes: "Humans." The job of taking care of the Great Lakes "belongs to all of us and I don't think we're aware of it," she said.

There is a simple way to start, she added. "I think an individual can recognize the majesty of the lakes and give them their due respect simply by visiting and showing praise for them."

I was starting to pick up a theme when asking whether friends and family talked about the Lakes. In Stephanie's case, "Yes, we do and it's mostly personal. They don't share the same love for the lakes as I do, but they have fond memories and they question the health of the lakes."

Nonetheless, she said she was "hopeful because I don't find it useful to be pessimistic."

"People care," she added, "but they don't necessarily know how to help. I don't think it's a priority for most people and perhaps we haven't found a way to effectively work together and collaborate."

Words from her Great Lakes Project website stuck with me. "There is incredible value in this sense of place," she had written there. "It kindles a spark for the Great Lakes and offers a peek into the depth of it all... inspiring us to live unsalted."

Even more to the point, and a direct answer to my recurrent question, was this from her site:

"'Knowledge is not self-executing'…I heard this phrase at a conference a few weeks ago in a talk about the need for more Great Lakes social science. It reminds me that all the science we do isn't enough if it isn't used in making decisions."

The speaker who had used the phrase told Stephanie, "I think it is relevant to your project because the connections and love of the lakes your work inspires is one of the ingredients we need to motivate knowledge to execution."

The need for inspiration – and the role of art in it – seemed one good lead in exploring the precarious state of the Lakes.

Interlude 10

You can live in one of the most water-wealthy regions of the world and know very little about its treasures.

Despite tens, if not hundreds of millions of dollars spent in the last three decades to infuse teaching about the environment into subject matter required on standardized tests, adults in the Great Lakes watershed are largely ignorant about such basic matters as where their drinking water comes from and where their sewage goes. In this regard they may be no worse than citizens in other regions, but those citizens don't live astride nearly one-fifth of the world's available surface freshwater. If there is a special stewardship responsibility for citizens of the Great Lakes watershed, relatively few are fulfilling it.

Sponsored by the International Joint Commission, two surveys of a total of about 8000 residents of the Great Lakes watershed in 2015 and 2018 are vivid illustrations. Citizens of all eight Great Lakes states and Ontario, the respondents had trouble answering simple questions.

Can you name anything that you feel may pose a threat to the lakes and rivers that surround and feed into the Great Lakes?

The leading answer in 2015, supplied by 24%, was "don't know." Next in line were invasive species, pollution in general, and garbage/waste with 23%, 13% and 8%, respectively. In 2018, "don't know" slipped down the list, coming in second after 26% for invasive species.

Can you tell me why you think that the Great Lakes need to be protected?

The leading answer in 2015, chosen by 23%, was "don't know." Following were drinking/household water at 20%, valuable resource at 19%, and four reasons tied at 6% -- sources for fresh water, for the fish/fishing, our health, and wildlife. In 2018, "don't know" was third at 17%, edged out by drinking/household water at 19% and valuable resource at 18%.

Can you tell me where your drinking water comes from?

In 2015, the second most frequently given answer (23%) was "don't know." It was third at 19% in 2018. Ground water sources such as wells or springs were the most common responses from 34% of those surveyed (33% in 2018); 20% said local lakes (21% in 2018). The Great Lakes or individual Great Lakes were named by a total of 19% of respondents. (The ratio of public drinking water supplies derived from groundwater to those derived from surface water on the U.S. side of the basin is roughly 25%-75%.)

Can you tell me where the waste water from your home usage goes?

The leading answer, "don't know," came from 31% of respondents. It also led the way at 28% in 2018. Septic systems were named by 17%, followed by a sewage plant by 13%, a waste water treatment facility by 11%, sewers by 7%, into local lakes or rivers by 7%, the ground or ground water sources by 4% and run off to fields or farm areas by 2%. A total of 8% named a Great Lake: Michigan (3%), Ontario (2%), Erie (1%), Huron (1%) and Superior (1%).

As the Commission pointed out, a "whopping" 88% thought it "important" or "very important (80%) that the health and water quality of the Great Lakes be protected, but it is difficult to protect what you don't understand. "Don't know" is a sobering refrain when uttered by substantial portions of a human community that should know much about the ecosystem they inhabit.

Chapter 10

I used to joke to Margaret (Marg) Schulte that when she died, she would arrive in heaven in the next instant. No stop lights on the way. She is that good a person. Not that she acts saintly. She conceals her good heart in wry sarcasm and small talk.

I met her around the State Capitol, where she was a legislative aide. Over the years that I knew her she worked for five different state representatives and senators that I can recall, loyally and uncomplainingly doing the casework that everyone else abhorred. She also has an astute policy brain.

Born in 1957, Marg spent her childhood in Scottville, Michigan, seven miles from Lake Michigan. But her early lake memories were 100 miles farther north, at the small historic fishing town of Leland, in the Leelanau Peninsula. Her mother had been born there.

"I was probably playing on the beach and in the water every day while we were up there," she said. "It didn't matter if it was sunny, cloudy, hot or cool. My siblings and I were down there always, unless it was thundering and lightning and then some of us, usually me and my brother Ferd, had to be dragged home and were pretty unhappy about it.

In the summer of 2015, Marg and her family observed the 10th anniversary of the death of Marg's oldest sister by flying kites on the beach in Ludington. "The breeze from Lake Michigan helped to send our kites soaring to the heavens. We felt her spirit with us."

The center of Marg's childhood, Ludington and Scottville, gave her family reasons to return ever year. "I make it up to Lake Michigan at least a couple of times each year. There is nothing quite like taking a walk along the shoreline, and if it's at least 60 degrees, I'll definitely take a swim. My love is Leland, and I used to spend my summer vacations up there, and did a lot of Petoskey stone searching and swimming on a daily basis."

Not surprisingly in light of that history, Marg said Lake Michigan was her favorite. "Big Blue has been my friend all of my life and I have always said, the west side is the best side."

Unsure about whether the Lakes were getting better or worse, Marg focused on two problems: invasive species and diversions of water outside the Great Lakes basin. The recent vote cast by Michigan Governor Rick Snyder in favor of a diversion project to benefit Waukesha, Wisconsin concerned her. "Thus begins a slippery slope." In the long run, with climate change accelerating, increasing the risk of lowered water levels, she feared diversions as the top threat to the Lakes.

"Most of my Michigan friends believe we have a treasure," Marg said. "Many of them live close to Lake Michigan and take advantage of all the opportunities, skiing, boating, swimming and just being on or near the lake. To be honest there isn't a lot of political talk, but there probably should be."

The state government of Michigan, given that it is surrounded by four of the Great Lakes, has the most to gain and the most to lose and should be the lead on their protection, she said. And then came a rare piece of profanity. "I think, over the years, Michigan has done a good job, but under this current administration, it's been pretty darn shitty."

If people care so much about the Great Lakes, why are they in mostly fair to poor condition? I asked Marg. "Most people don't see that, and probably won't care until it's very visible. Like when parts of Lake Erie were on fire, folks could see that there was definitely a problem."

So there: another vote cast for slow-motion, nearly invisible deterioration as the reason the lakes weren't rallying more defenders.

Interlude 10

Intending to move away from the shore no more than six months after arriving, I stayed longer. It was not a decision, but an indecision. Inertia paradoxically is the strongest force in many lives, including my own.

The charms of Lake Huron began to seduce me. The beat, for one thing. It was an unusual year in that even in mid-summer the northeast wind frequently rose and drove the lake into the beach tirelessly. At times the pounding went on for several days and nights. The repetition was comfort; the way a rocking cradle is to a baby. Once in a while I wished for it to cease, but more frequently I was glad about the reminder of the lake – of the fact that I didn't live in the mundane nearly lake-free country around Lansing, my residence for many years. This was special territory.

The romance of the scenic vista was nothing new. It had comforted me from the anxious day of my arrival in August 2015. But now I absorbed it, took it into me. At mid-afternoon of many summer days, the water was a wholesome deep blue while cumulus clouds ascended into the paler blue above. In the presence of this scene, my early youth became vividly real to me, recalling a time when the future bore a seemingly inexhaustible supply of benign summer days.

Upon moving in, I had felt slightly overwhelmed by the visitors who occupied the small beach. Circumstances had rendered seclusion not just a comfort, but an absolute necessity. But now I valued the joyous screams of kids romping in the waves, the sight of fathers and mothers aiding their toddlers into the shallows or hoisting them upon their shoulders, fashioning the kind of memories I carried with me after a half century.

The freighters became familiar. A few of them passed through often enough that their names were recognizable – the John B. Aird a prime example. Christened in 1983 in honor of the lieutenant (pronounced left-tenant by the Canadians) governor of Ontario, the 730-footer often carried coal, iron ore or taconite pellets – or so said boatnerd.com.

Sometimes the passage of the freighters was easily discerned without the faculty of sight – the "whoob, whoob, whoob" of the propeller blades pulsed across the water and seemingly into the ground beneath me. Other times they glided past in ghostly silence. Often in the deep of night, the lights of freighters were discernible as the faintest of glimmerings on the horizon to the north, and these were too far away to make any sound.

It's commonplace to say a lake has many moods and colors, but it was the moods of the beach that increasingly pleased me. Just after sunrise it was dull and still like an awakening person. At the height of day, it was a blazing stage for summer dreams. In the evening it slowly released the heat of the day, like a runner catching his breath at race's end.

The lake may have been most beautiful to me when I could barely see it. It lacked the menace of the midnight lake in winter, when the heaving waves a few yards away threatened death. In summer, even when disturbed, the lake was life giving rather than taking. More often ripples of light from the Ontario towns to the southeast illuminated a quietly busy lake; it seemed to be purposeful, but about what I didn't know.

When it was completely still in the late of night and the moon was absent, the panorama of constellations shifted imperceptibly but decisively over the lake. This time the lake was a stage for the drama of the heavens.

One night that summer I returned from out of town after 2:30 a.m. My vacation had four more days to run. It seemed a shame to waste a good dawn. I stayed up reading, every now and then walking out the back door to see whether first light had come up over the lake. The first half dozen times it had not. Finally, a flap in the sky pulled up from the horizon like a window shade. The lake this July morning was in deep sleep, its wash against the shore barely a murmur.

The advent of day was bittersweet. If only the progress of the light could halt for several hours so the pale blue just above the reddish-orange at the horizon could continue to mingle at its back edge with the blue-black of night. This private showing was a humbling gift. But I managed to be greedy, wanting it to persist. Unconcerned with my preferences, Thursday morning broke with the sun's climb over the horizon. It was a bleary light, a sun still struggling to awaken.

And yet its appearance was a triumph. Having watched the entire process of night becoming day, I felt as though I had helped the sun up a ladder and shoved it over the top of a watery wall. Now the lake was liquid silver, like the mercury that, in methylated form, plagues fish and fish consumers in every corner of the Great Lakes watershed. But this molten silver was startlingly beautiful.

Of all the phases of day, however, the lake looked most fetching to me in the evening. The mood that comes with the conclusion of a day's labor often mirrored Huron's demeanor. The waves often subsided and their splashing dwindled to a sigh. On those evenings merely standing in the lake's presence was healing. It had seen 9,000 years of sunrises and sunsets and was still vital.

My affection for and attachment to the lake reached the point where I regretted the frequent necessity of turning away from it for trips inland or down to Detroit. This is where I wanted to be.

Chapter 11

Alex Mayer is one of those brilliant men who keep a low profile, lest they be damned with fervent praise. Humble and quiet, he knows water – the water of Sonora, Mexico and the water of the Great Lakes. A professor at Michigan Technological University in Houghton, he was director of the Center for Water and Society there and a professor of civil and environmental engineering. Over the years I had spoken to his students and worked with him on Great Lakes projects in both the non-profit and governmental sectors.

An Atlanta boy by birth, he lived in Georgia for 9 years, San Diego for 9 years, Rhode Island for 4 years, Berkeley for 4 years and North Carolina for 6 years before coming to MTU. He had now lived in the university community Houghton/Hancock Michigan for 25 years. Before becoming a professor, he worked as a planning engineer for a municipal water and wastewater agency for 4 years in Oakland, California.

Despite growing up in the South, he had an early Great Lakes memory -- the winter wind off of Lake Michigan in downtown Chicago. "I was about 6 years old, visiting my grandmother from Atlanta, and I was not pleased with the cold," he said. "But, 16 years later, I was traveling along the north shore of Lake Superior in the summer, driving back to California. The lake was too much to take in all at once, and so were the unending tracts of northern forest. Still, it really took moving here, next to Lake Superior, another 13 years later, to appreciate the whole thing."

The lake was always nearby now. A few weeks before I interviewed him, he had taken a walk on the beach. "Gorgeous as usual. We said, 'why don't we do this more often?'"

Alex was an expert who read plenty of academic papers and conversed regularly with other scientists and government officials. I asked him for his read on the state of the Great Lakes. "I would say some things are getting better, but others worse. I'm concerned about our ability to predict or manage against exotic species. I'm concerned that the Lakes are still acting as reservoirs for emerging contaminants. And, I'm concerned that we're not ready to adapt to the Great Lakes." He was unequivocal that exotic species were the biggest menace to the Great Lakes.

Alex thought "informed, organized citizens can put pressure on local to national level policy-makers. We should all do our best to communicate what we think is going in on in the Great Lakes, not only to our colleagues, but the greater public." He cited as reason for optimism about the Great Lakes "a slow shift towards more protection and restoration," then added, "but what do I know?"

Interestingly, in thinking about Great Lakes conversations, Alex noted two types. "My academic friends talk about science issues, all of which are important, but my nonacademic friends worry about water diversions, exotic species invasion, unfettered access to recreation on the lakes and the tributary watersheds. They also talk about frustration with politics in general, and they're pessimistic about government, especially federal, ever getting anything done with respect to the Great Lakes."

I jumped around with my questions, asking him now if he had a favorite Great Lake. Instead of saying "Superior," he replied, "I'm stunned by all of the Lakes and wish I knew them all better."

He said the question of government roles in protecting the Great Lakes was complicated, since international, national, state/provincial, municipal governments and "everything in between" have responsibility. "Plus citizens need to vote for people that they think will protect the Great Lakes. Scientists and policymakers need to work together to come up with smart strategies," he said.

To my standard question of why the Lakes were in trouble when so many people deeply cared about them, Alex mused, "Perhaps the messages we're sending people are too foreboding and complex and we haven't found the right way to communicate. Also, people take the Great Lakes for granted as long as there isn't green scum washing up on the shore."

Scientist Alex and Policy Advisor Dave agreed on Alex's final thought. "We have to invest in monitoring to see if whatever we're doing to protect or restore the Lakes is working.". But as we both knew, politicians find monitoring less than glamorous, even wasteful, and cut it very early in lean times. It's like throwing your road map out the car window to lighten your load and make the gasoline last longer.

Interlude 11

Polls often say environmental issues are important to a majority of voters, but it's difficult to identify a single officeholder at the state or federal level who owes her or his election to clean air and water and all the associated issues. Certainly, no president has captured the White House primarily on the strength of progressive environmental stands.

When Barack Obama won the 2008 election, the environment wasn't in the top tier of issues. The U.S. economy was toppling into a near-depression and fear characterized the electorate. Still, during his campaign, Great Lakes state candidate Obama of Illinois had promised a major budget commitment to Great Lakes restoration – $5 billion in new funding. How this pledge ended up in his platform, how it was sold to Congress after he was elected and what became of it tell us a great deal about the gap between the public's love of the lakes and their knowledge of the actions undertaken in their name.

The proximate cause of the Obama pledge was a Great Lakes initiative undertaken in the name of President George W. Bush. Needing the electoral votes of Great Lakes states in his 2004 re-election attempt, and taking punishing criticism for his environmental record, Bush – under the tutelage of his Environmental Protection Agency Administrator, Michael Leavitt – signed an executive order declaring the Great Lakes "a national treasure." Inked in May 2004, the order set in motion something called "a regional collaboration of national significance." Essentially, the order called for a host of federal agencies to work with the proverbial "stakeholders" to write a document setting priorities for federal funding and other actions to restore the Great Lakes. At a summit meeting in Chicago in December 2004, Leavitt organized a drum-and-bagpipes procession preceding the signing by the many participants of a Great Lakes Declaration articulating their commitment to work on a strategy.

By then, Bush had won re-election and the need for Great Lakes state electoral votes had passed. So, when over 1,500 government and non-government Collaboration participants produced a $20 billion Great Lakes Regional Collaboration Strategy that was unveiled at another Chicago meeting in December 2005 (at which attendees signed yet another declaration), it led to virtually no actions and no new funding. Some advocates felt hoodwinked. They vowed to challenge the major party candidates in 2008 to make commitments to fund the strategy's key features.

A resident of Chicago, and in a neighborhood only a few blocks from Lake Michigan, Obama knew and cared enough about the Great Lakes to fulfill the hopes of the advocates. Those same advocates had a tool to deploy in support of the new president's Great Lakes budget – public opinion surveys. The Healing Our Waters – Great Lakes Coalition periodically released polls showing a strong majority of respondents in the Great Lakes states favored increased federal funding for restoration of the ecosystem. The same coalition rolled out – and over the years, stuck with – the message to the public that the Great Lakes, among other things, were an important source of drinking water and now was not the time to neglect investment.

A closer look at one of the surveys is instructive. Released a month before the 2012 election, a survey of Wisconsin voters performed for the Coalition found that 75%, including 63% of Republicans and 84% of Democrats, supported continuing federal government funding for Great Lakes restoration. The affirmations weren't surprising in light of the question:

"Over the last three years, the U.S. federal government has spent $300 million a year to improve the condition of the Great Lakes by cleaning up toxic waste and bacteria, reducing runoff pollution from cities and farms, and protecting and rebuilding wetlands. In your opinion, should the federal government continue that funding for Great Lakes restoration or should it reduce the funding?"

Not many would support increased toxic waste and bacteria.

In fact, other state surveys undertaken on behalf of the Coalition yielded almost the same findings, no matter how conservative or liberal its electorate might be. A 2012 Ohio survey found 72% supported continuing Great Lakes restoration funding and 54% rejected the idea that such funding should take a budget cut "along with everything else."

Despite the good intentions of the Coalition and its member groups, the surveys, and other evidence proffered of public support, told us very little about what voters knew or how much they cared about the Great Lakes. They were a gauge of mostly first impressions of voters who hadn't known there was something called the Great Lakes Restoration Initiative or GLRI, funded by Obama at $475 million in 2009-10 and approximately $300 million a year after that. Explained to them in the most fundamental and flattering terms, the GLRI predictably had appeal. How could it not?

As had been the case since the dawn of the environmental movement, advocates were acting as proxies for the public in lobbying Congress to continue Great Lakes restoration funding. This time they were armed with numbers associated with the politician's passport to success – a public opinion survey. But it did not necessarily mean that they had the public behind them in more than the most general way.

Still, perhaps more enamored of the surveys than they should have been, members of Congress kept the money flowing, often adding money to GLRI that Obama proposed cutting. The money resulted in some significant improvements, including the cleanup of contaminated hotspots in Great Lakes bays and harbors. But it did nothing to restrain the collapse of western Lake Erie into a plague of harmful algal blooms each summer.

.

Chapter 12

One of the most philosophical and generous men I've ever known is Tom Bailey. Son of a renowned state Department of Natural Resources wildlife biologist, Tom himself has had a distinguished conservation career. He was a park ranger at Grand Portage National Monument and Isle Royale National Park, an employee of the DNR water quality program and, most importantly, an employee and executive director of the Little Traverse Conservancy, a land trust, for 30 years.

He's also a first-rate host, and I have stayed several times at his house in Petoskey, greedily attacking his breakfasts and dinners. He's a Republican and I'm not. Ordinarily, our dogma yielded to our shared belief in conservation.

To all of his work he has brought a keen eye and intelligence, and he has now authored a monumental collection of essays that were bound for book publication at the time we communicated. I knew he would be an unusually articulate interview.

Tom was 62 and deeply proud of his son John, who had served in the infantry in Afghanistan, graduated from Central Michigan University, and now worked for Huron Pines, a nonprofit organization in northeastern Lower Michigan, setting rivers free through dam removal projects and road-stream crossing improvements.

Tom's early Great Lakes memories reached back to the days before completion of the Mackinac Bridge in 1957. He also remembered spending time with friends on Lake Superior when young. The Baileys made several trips to the Les Cheneaux Islands, off the southeastern shores of the Upper Peninsula, where they rented a cabin and fished for perch in Lake Huron. "I always loved the Big Water, the sand dunes, and watching the freighters," he said. "When we had the chance to move to Marquette, I absolutely loved it."

"My first aerial view [of the Great Lakes] was flying by seaplane to Isle Royale when I was 15. I could see clear across the Lake—from Thunder Bay and the Sleeping Giant in Canada, across Isle Royale, and to the Keweenaw Peninsula and even the Huron Mountains beyond. It was spectacular."

At 17, Tom beheld different conditions on his first commercial jet plane flight -- to Washington, D.C. to testify before the Senate Interior Committee on an Isle Royale wilderness proposal he had helped to develop. "Flying over Lake Erie," he said, "I was struck by all the pollution. Large areas of the Lake were covered in some kind of foam or scum or floating debris. Large areas were discolored. It was quite a shock after growing up on the relatively clean waters of Lake Superior."

Not long before the interview, he had visited a friend's private beach on the Lake Michigan shore. The image stuck.

"A sailboat had run aground, and we went to see the wreck. It was blowing a stiff breeze out of the northwest, and the September sky had all the look of fall. We looked out toward Skillagalee, with Beaver and Hog Islands off to the west, and Waugoshance Island in Wilderness State Park to the north. The boat was a little over 30 feet long and had washed up to the area where the waves were breaking. It was resting on its side and its long keel. The sunset was spectacular, and the scene had a surreal quality to it."

Tom's acquaintance with the Great Lakes was intimate. He saw Lake Michigan every day, just as he had seen Lake Superior every day while growing up in Marquette.

He owns what he called a "shack on the Lake" north of Cross Village that looks out over the Beaver Island archipelago and the chain of Islands at Wilderness State Park. "There's a 40-foot bluff that offers a commanding view, he said. "I love to watch the gulls and terns during the day, see the occasional bald eagle soaring above or fishing on the Lake, and watch the sunset."

The Great Lakes were an everyday part of his conservancy work. "We're mainly concerned about protecting the land that keeps the Lakes healthy. Marshes and wetlands are a particular priority. We do talk occasionally about the politics, and things like funding priorities for conservation programs," he said.

Tom has read widely. He said he enjoyed works like Jerry Dennis' *The Living Great* Lakes. "I've had a number of coffee table books about Lake Superior, and also read Rolf Peterson's work about the wolves of Isle Royale. I've read a couple of mystery novels about the Great Lakes, including one about some shipwrecks off Isle Royale that were actually explored while I was a Park Ranger there.

I asked him to sum up his feelings about the Lakes in a sentence and a word. Sentence:
"One of the most remarkable natural areas and natural resources on the face of the Earth." I Word: "Precious."

He saw complexity when I asked him if the Lakes were improving or deteriorating. "They're better in some ways—the tanneries that dumped huge amounts of waste are all gone and industrial discharges have been dramatically reduced. Municipal wastewater is better controlled than before. But there are still problems: hormones, drugs, micro-plastics, airborne mercury and other pollutants present hazards. Agricultural runoff is still a big problem as are combined sewer overflows."

The biology of the Lakes, he said, had been "ravaged by invasive species. The Great Lakes aquatic ecosystem amounts to a huge science experiment right now, with little or no control on outside inputs."

Who was accountable for these problems? "That's the crux of the problem: there is no one lead responsible party. There are two nations, eight states…it's confusing and there are overlapping jurisdictions and also holes."

Tom's experience successfully promoting the Isle Royale wilderness legislation in Congress as "a kid from Marquette" had bred a lasting belief that individuals can make a difference.

"Each one of us can learn, speak out, and control our own behaviors. Urge your governmental units to clean up wastewater, to control storm water discharges. Support control of agricultural runoff pollution. Don't buy products with microplastics. Vote for candidates who will respect and protect the lakes. Talk to your friends."

So why weren't the Lakes getting better? "Money, pure and simple. Politics and policy are money-driven."

His sunny optimism faded a bit when I asked about the future. He ticked off the challenges: runaway population growth, increasing pressure for water from arid regions, climate change, invasive species, and more.

"I can't really say whether the future is more bright or more cloudy, because my time to affect it is growing short," he mused. "I'm in the sunset years, and it will be up to the next generations to take over. I'm confident when I see people like my son working to protect our natural resources, but when I look at the growing mass of urbanized humanity that has no clue about nature and no personal link to the outdoors, I worry about the future.

"I fear that people like my father, like me and like my son—people who grow up outdoors, and hunt and fish, and camp and learn about nature firsthand and then go on not only to enjoy the outdoors but to help others enjoy and protect it – are a dying breed."

Interlude 12

If someone mentioned a nonpoint issue to you, and you weren't immersed in environmental policy, you might correct her and say she means a pointless issue. But she meant what she said.

Could it be that the Great Lakes are in peril, even deteriorating in spite of the public's professed embrace of them, in part because environmental lawyers and advocates have created a dialect that many citizens can't understand?

A paramount is example is "nonpoint," as in nonpoint source pollution. Those in the field use this term, plucked from the U.S. Clean Water Act, to refer to the fraction of pollution that does not come from concentrated points like sewage plants and factories. Nonpoint source pollution is diffuse, usually running off farmland or city streets into rivers and lakes. How many people whom you encounter in your everyday life could define "nonpoint source pollution"?

That's only the beginning. The point sources must receive Clean Water Act permits, or NPDES permits. NPDES is a quaint acronym whose origins are almost lost in the mists of 46-year-old history. It stands for "national pollution discharge elimination system." The authors of the 1972 Act envisioned a system of permits that would ultimately promote the end of pollution discharges to America's lakes and streams.

There are more water-related terms in environmental jargon, some more accessible than others. Factories and sewage plants don't discharge pollution, they release effluent. And sewage plants aren't called that; they're wastewater treatment facilities.

The circle of Great Lakes code ripples outward, baffling and perhaps deterring participation by those outside the elite waters of environmental regulation and advocacy.

And then there are the bewildering acronyms. A sample includes:

- *GLWQA – Great Lakes Water Quality Agreement. Inked by Canadian Prime Minister Pierre Trudeau and U.S. President Richard Nixon in 1972, the Agreement guides binational policy to protect and manage the water quality of the Lakes. The two nations renegotiated the GLWQA in 1978, 1987 and 2012.*

- *GLEC – Great Lakes Executive Committee. Established by the Great Lakes Water Quality Agreement, this body consists of representatives from 12 Canadian agencies, 11 U.S. agencies (and more sub-agencies), the Province of Ontario, the Great Lakes states, Tribes, First Nations, Metis, municipalities and others, and has a charge of helping "coordinate, implement, review and report on programs, practices and measures undertaken to achieve the purpose" of the GLWQA.*

- *GLRI – Great Lakes Restoration Initiative. Launched by the Obama Administration in 2009, it is the special federal funding program for Great Lakes protection grants.*

- *GLC – Great Lakes Commission. This interstate compact organization consists of representatives from the eight Great Lakes states, while observers from Ontario and Quebec participate without vote in its meetings. It has no authority but attracts attention for conducting studies and organizing the states around common positions on environmental and transportation issues.*

- *GLFC – Great Lakes Fishery Commission. Established by a 1955 convention between the U.S. and Canada, the Commission superintends sea lamprey control and promotes coordinated management of Great Lakes fisheries. It has no authority but is regarded as a smooth-functioning organization helpful to the states, Ontario and federal agencies charged with lamprey control.*

- *GLPA – Great Lakes Protection Act. The act, which received final approval in November 2015, is a framework for Great Lakes work undertaken by the Province of Ontario.*

- *GLAB – Great Lakes Advisory Board. The Board advises U.S. EPA on implementation of the GLRI.*

- *GLOS – Great Lakes Observing System. GLOS is a nonprofit organization that promotes "a coordinated network of people, equipment and technology working together to provide data about the Great Lakes in a variety of formats and applications" and provides "data services to support the region's need for data, modeling, and other data tools or products."*

- *GLAM – Great Lakes Adaptive Management Committee. The International Joint Commission created this panel to assist boards controlling the outflow of water in the St. Marys, Niagara and St. Lawrence Rivers to undertake "the monitoring, modeling and assessment necessary for evaluating regulation plans and address other questions that may arise due to changing conditions." Changing climate and its unpredictable effect on water levels is a primary force behind the committee's creation.*

- *GLNI -- Great Lakes Nutrient Initiative. A program launched by Environment Canada (now Environment Canada and Climate Change), it spent $16 million to identify sources of nutrients feeding Lake Erie algae blooms and develop strategies and objectives to reduce them.*

- *GLERL – Great Lakes Environmental Research Laboratory. Located near Ann Arbor, Michigan, the lab is one of several U.S. federal agency laboratories dedicated to Great Lakes science. It is part of the National Oceanic and Atmospheric Administration.*

And those are just some of the acronyms that begin with "GL." There is a multitude of Great Lakes acronyms and institutions, requiring a map for outsiders to navigate.

Citizens often ask, "Who's in charge of the Great Lakes?" They assume a supreme body somewhere oversees and governs the Great Lakes. But it's a complex natural ecosystem, and an even more complex ecosystem of governance, with two federal governments, eight states, two provinces, tribes, First Nations and Metis, and over 2000 municipalities, just for starters. The question is whether it is so complex that it deters the public from participating in Great Lakes management.

Chapter 13

How do you interview your brother? There's no quick answer, but if I'm trying to learn from people who love the Great Lakes it would be a great oversight not to interview Thomas Dempsey. I don't know many people who love them with a purer heart than my younger brother. He's in quiet bliss when anticipating, experiencing or reflecting on a day at a Lake Michigan beach.

Tom has a piercing intellect and a distaste for cant. I got what I expected – crisp, well-considered answers and observations.

Because we're three years apart, his first Great Lakes memory was inevitably different from mine. But the memory he cited was from age 8 or 9. "My family [he wrote as if just another interviewee] drove to the Upper Peninsula one winter to visit my grandfather or grandmother. I remember looking at the ice floes on Lake Michigan from the car as we drove along US 2. It's my first conscious memory of the Lakes—Lake Michigan looked cold and endless."

A more recent memory involved Lakeport State Park, five miles north of where I lived, where he stationed himself on occasional summer visits.

"I spent several mornings on a deserted state park beach on Lake Huron," he wrote. "I enjoy experiencing the summertime beauty of the Great Lakes—the sun, sand, water and wind—at all times of the day, but there's something special about enjoying the Lakes on a beautiful morning when no one is around. It's a memory I know I'll look back on during the approaching long winter months, a feeling of beauty and serenity."

I asked him whether he thought Great Lakes are getting better, worse or staying about the same – and what helped him form that opinion.

"It's difficult for the average person to answer that question. All I know is what I read in the papers and hear on the radio and TV, but there don't seem to be that many stories about the Great Lakes these days. My hunch is that things are getting worse, because politicians don't seem to be that concerned about the Great Lakes, yet the Great Lakes face new challenges, like climate change and the threat posed by Asian carp and farm runoff.

Asked to name the biggest threat to the lakes, he hit first on climate change, then corrected himself to say, "maybe the biggest threat is the selfishness on the part of the special interests who pollute the lakes and buy off politicians."

Tom wasn't enthusiastic about individual actions as the cure for what ailed the lakes. He said voting for candidates who support Great Lakes causes and walking instead of driving could help in a small way.

"But if I were a farmer discharging phosphorous into Lake Erie, I know for sure that I could do something to benefit the Great Lakes!"

He was much more sanguine about the future of the Great Lakes – in the long run. "It seems as though human beings careen toward disaster until the last minute, then make the necessary course correction—that seems to be our nature. And the value of the Great Lakes is so apparent, that, in the end, I think we will save them from us."

His next response fit an emerging pattern. The Lakes were not only not on every Michigander's mind, but also never seen by many of them. "My friends never visit the Great Lakes, and they never talk about them, either. And though I encourage them to visit them in the summer, they never do. But we're lucky, because there are plenty of inland lakes in Michigan for anyone to visit."

Lake Michigan was his baby. "There's something about the wide, sandy beaches and the sunsets that, to me, make Lake Michigan the greatest Great Lake," he said.

His quarrel with the way government protected the Great Lakes was not with the agencies but with the assumptions behind the laws they enforced. Instead of eliminating pollution they were expected to limit it.

"We've accepted that it's okay for industry to belch their poisons into our air and water, and that concerns me. There's no media coverage questioning that premise."

He issued two powerful indictments. The first followed my standard question about why the Lakes were deteriorating in spite of public support.

He wrote, "I think people are lazy. We want our leaders to protect the Great Lakes and we leave that problem in their hands. But the state of the Great Lakes is not people's everyday concern, it's more of an abstract concern. It's probably only something we think about when we actually visit the beach in the summer and find debris in the water, or see headlines about algal blooms in Lake Erie. Meanwhile, the Great Lakes are under constant attack from industry and budget-cutting fiscal conservatives."

The second was spontaneous. He lamented, and then expressed relief, that the Lakes didn't get more national attention. "Maybe that's a good thing—as long as people aren't aware of the tremendous resource they represent, they won't try to divert them or move here to enjoy their summers on the Great Lakes. But we don't celebrate the Great Lakes on a national level or even seem to appreciate them particularly."

Tom wasn't the first, nor would he be the last, to suggest the Lakes were taken for granted by those living close to them. He was not guilty of that. He dreamed all winter, and planned all summer, about carefree days relating quietly and in privacy when possible to Lake Michigan or Huron.

DAVE DEMPSEY

Interlude 13

Not long ago I sat in an Ontario theater for the Canadian premiere of an American-produced Great Lakes film. Although entertaining and informative, the movie left me a little queasy, and I wasn't sure why. Then the explanation tapped me on the shoulder like a polite Canadian: the film had exactly zero Canadian characters. It was almost as though the Great Lakes shores of Canada were unpopulated. Even the fact that it took me 45 minutes to recognize their absence marked me as a true American. Is it any wonder why Canadians value two binational institutions, the Great Lakes Fishery Commission and the International Joint Commission, which have equal representation for the two nations?

One of the fundamental values of Great Lakes stewardship must be respect across the aquatic U.S.-Canadian border. The nation to the south has roughly ten times the population of its partner, but not ten times the wisdom. A profound concern for sensible protection characterizes both.

There is some historical reason, in fact, to believe the Canadians were first in Great Lakes conservation. The legendary Canadian scientist Henry Regier noted that Canadian and U.S. approaches to the Great Lakes fishery in the 1800s were sharply opposed, leading to international tensions, and that this might be traceable to the nations' respective origins.

"Did the personal freedoms that came with the [American] Revolution implicitly support laissez-faire extraction related to fishery and other natural resources?" he asked. "If so, would this be another instance of 'revolution devouring its own'? Meanwhile in Canada, especially as related to Great Lakes Basin fisheries, an implicit commitment to conservation came automatically as Britain transferred much of its governance traditions to colonies in the Empire."

It is undeniably true that the U.S. moved to regulate Great Lakes fishing and the fishery well after Canada. While not romanticizing the Canadians as unfailing Great Lakes guardians, Americans would do well to recognize the ways in which Canadians have championed the Great Lakes.

Canadian scientists, for example, were instrumental in the work that led to the 1972 Great Lakes Water Quality Agreement and to the promotion of ecosystem principles that shaped the 1978 revision of the Agreement.

Even the government of Prime Minister Stephen Harper, regarded by some as hostile to environmental protection, thought big in at least one act of Great Lakes conservation. The Harper regime declared a 3,800-square mile swath – almost half – of the Canadian waters of Lake Superior a National Marine Conservation Area in 2015. In essence an aquatic national park, the designation is the strongest the national government can impose, prohibiting mining, dumping and oil and gas exploration and extraction. It's designed to permit regulated fishing and promote low-impact recreation. Perhaps most important, it acknowledges the unparalleled quality of the largest Great Lake and the value of perpetuating it far into the future.

At this writing, the closest thing to the National Marine Conservation Area on the U.S. side was the Thunder Bay National Marine Sanctuary in Michigan's waters of Lake Huron (although other sanctuary proposals were beginning to crawl through the designation process). The 4,300-square mile Sanctuary was authorized for shipwreck protection, which, despite expanded environmental education efforts, remains its primary raison d'etre. While shipwrecks are an important part of Great Lakes history and maritime lore, their protection has only secondary environmental value.

The point is not to denigrate American Great Lakes protection efforts, but to underscore the Canadian. The dogma of American exceptionalism has too often been a shield against the uncomfortable truth that other nations have something to teach the U.S., in this case about environmental stewardship.

Binationalism is critical, but it can't be forgotten that many nations exist among the Lakes, including First Nations and Tribes. Each of them is a sovereign with rights to the resources and an inherent role in their governance.

While Americans may forget that other nations share responsibility for conserving and managing the Great Lakes, these water bodies can't differentiate among nations and their natural resource regimes. Like the water draining from their respective lands, the effects of U.S. and Canadian Great Lakes policies blend in one world-class pool. It is lucky for the Lakes that Canada is a full and equal partner in their conservation. More so after the 2016 U.S. election.

Chapter 14

You can hear Grant Jewett Merritt a mile off. His gravelly voice reminds you of a power saw revving up. It generally conveys bonhomie. But that doesn't mean its owner has shunned conflict.

Descended from the Merritt men who opened Minnesota's Iron Range, Grant grew up in Duluth, close to Lake Superior. In fact, in his autobiography, he describes watching freighters on Lake Superior through his high school window. Without the greatest of the Great Lakes, the Merritt brothers' ore find would have had a much more difficult time getting to mills – and Grant would not have made environmental history.

Appointed by Governor Wendell Anderson to run the Minnesota Pollution Control Agency in 1971, Grant immediately challenged the Reserve Mining Company, whose taconite tailing wastes from its Silver Bay, Minnesota plant had not only formed an ugly delta immediately along the shore, but also drifted into Wisconsin and Michigan waters. An estimated 67,000 tons *per day* of waste was dumped in the lake.

He had targeted the company since a visit from his uncle Milton Mattson in 1967. He recorded the information in his journal:

"The slag and pollution can be seen in the water as far west as Two Harbors. It collects on the bottom and kills fish eggs in spawning grounds. Milton says it goes across to the south shore as well. Reserve Mining has been hoodwinking the public recently, since the newspaper publicity, Milton said. For instance, it has called the picture of the slag in the Sunday *Minneapolis Tribune* an 'illusion.' Second, when Reserve heard that Secretary of the Interior Udall was going to fly over the delta and plant buildings, they 'seeded' the slag with grass seed—thus temporarily turning the area green—now, of course, it is back to the dirty brown."

He was now hooked on doing something to stop Reserve's appalling pollution of Lake Superior. His journal entry concludes: "The only way to force Reserve is to apply political pressure. Milton tells me Reserve is doing nothing to solve it, when obviously something could be done."

It was a classic jobs v. environment battle. Neither Grant nor his boss, the governor, flinched. They cajoled, enforced and successfully urged U.S. EPA to sue. Citizens rallied. The press exposed. The result, after more than a decade, was a monumental victory for clean water. The company agreed to dispose of the wastes in an inland pond. The Minnesota Historical Society says: "The ruling in *The United States of America v. Reserve Mining Company* was considered a landmark decision. It gave the EPA broader powers to regulate corporate pollution, a practice unheard of before the lawsuit."

Grant was 83 when I interviewed him, but I'd known him for a decade by then. He'd told me a lot of war stories from the environmental front.

Lake Superior starred in his early memories: Picnics along the North Shore of Lake Superior at Gooseberry State Park and at age 5 taking the passenger boat *Winyah* from Grand Marais, Minnesota to Tobin Harbor in Isle Royale National Park.

"As we left after three weeks at our island the Captain let me blow the *Winyah*'s whistle for the next stop at Rock Harbor Lodge. That was quite a thrill," he said.

The thrills continued more than 75 years later. Grant's family was one of the relatively few private property owners, also known as inholders, in the national park. The rustic cabin had been in the clan for generations.

"Last summer my family and I made our annual Lake Superior trip from Tobin Harbor, Isle Royale, about 7 miles east. We pulled our two boats into the beach at the east end of Passage Island. That's the most easterly of the Isle Royale islands that surround the main island. We beach combed, had a picnic, waded along the shoreline and then went fishing. That was on the reefs that extend towards the Gull Islands four miles farther east along the Canadian boundary line."

Grant said the "park folks" estimated 400 islands were scattered around the 45-mile-long main island, and that the family explored their shores every year.

He took a positive view on the health of the lake he knew best. Lake Superior was getting somewhat better, he said, due to citizen pressure and the resulting response of politicians. But lack of enforcement had resulted in the onslaught of invasive species plaguing all the Great Lakes.

"The fishing in Lake Superior has recovered after the lamprey and smelt wreaked havoc with the lake trout and herring populations. The result is a mix of improvement and back sliding."

He was unequivocal about the biggest threat to the lakes: "Climate change. It's causing air pollution, adverse effects on lake levels and reduced visibility."

It was heartening that an octogenarian with more than 50 years' experience in the environmental field believed in individual action. It "can cause real change. Joining
with other citizen activists to champion clean water and air is crucial."

He recalled approvingly the citizen group Save Lake Superior Association, which he helped found in the 1960s, and which had successfully fought Reserve Mining and helped bring about other improvements in Lake Superior.

Grant continued in the positive vein when I asked him for his view on the future of the Lakes: "Hopeful, because many more people and organizations are watching and acting to preserve the waters and environs of the Great Lakes."

Unlike many I interviewed, Grant affirmed that he and friends often conversed about the Lakes. "Yes we do. Personal conversations and acts to improve the waters and areas around the Great Lakes. We talk about the fishing and waters. We talk about what various governmental units are doing and we talk about specific issues such as what Enbridge pipelines may do to pollute the Lakes."

He acknowledged caring "more about Lake Superior because I spend a good deal of time there. I do care about the other four Great Lakes because of what I read is happening or not happening with them." A telltale sign of his interests was his Great Lakes reading list: *Shipwrecks of Lake Superior* by Julius Fred Wolff, Jr.; *This Vast Pollution,* by Thomas Bastow; *Lake Superior Story and Spirit* by John and Ann Mahan; *The Great Lakes North America's Inland Sea* by Outdoor World; *The Great Lakes Reader* by Walter Havighurst; and *North Shore: A Natural History of Minnesota's Superior Shore* by Anderson and Fischer.

As a former state official, Grant assigned lead responsibility for managing the lakes to the eight Great Lakes states and Ontario, then the federal governments of Canada and the United States. "They could all do a better job. The International Joint Commission often prods the governments to do a better job, which is a good idea."

He had a ready answer to the reason for the mediocre state of the Lakes. "The politicians need more pushing and prodding." His advice to advocates: "Just keep pushing!"

If he said it after decades of advocacy – if he thought it made a difference – how could we not listen?

Interlude 14

It began somewhere back in the thick mists of time, probably in the late 1970s. Hundreds of people climbed into inner tubes, pushed off from Lighthouse Beach in Port Huron, Michigan, and floated six miles downstream to Marysville, Michigan. More than a few lashed six-packs of beer to their tubes. The tubers laid back, smiled, and allowed themselves to be ushered downstream by the swift current of the St. Clair River.

What came to be called the Float Down occurred annually. Even in its nascent days, hazards would have undermined the fun had the floaters paid attention. Thick freighter traffic menaced them; alcohol fogged their faculties. But no one was seriously injured, no one died.

Until 2014. That year, the Float Down sustained its first casualty by drowning. Unhappy with the event from the beginning, local authorities hoped the fatality would steer Float Down participants away. Instead, the event continued to grow despite the lack of official sanction and formal organization. No one was in charge, so no one could call the event off.

The sole website for the event, which offered helpful advice like "Stay out of the shipping channel, You vs. a Ship, you will lose every time," was careful to state that its owners were "in no way organizing, sponsoring, planning, or promoting a community event in any form. This site is maintained as a source of information and as a community service."

The advice about the shipping channel had become superfluous. To reduce the risk of fatalities, the Coast Guard had shut down freighter traffic for the duration of the Float Down, until approximately 8 p.m. The gain in safety was a loss in profit for shippers.

In 2016, Float Down Day, August 21, dawned benignly. A late summer sun rapidly warmed the air and anyone who had not consulted the weather forecast had reason to believe in an idyllic day. But that forecast called for a chance of afternoon showers, and more significantly, increasing winds.

Approximately at the informally scheduled time of 1 p.m., the floaters began setting forth from Lighthouse Beach. First a few at irregular intervals, soon a steady flow of people and their makeshift vessels. The participants really weren't tubers any more, not most of them. A large number had bought water mattresses or rafts for the ride to Marysville. At least two had erected bicycles on top of their mattresses and pedaled downstream. They were fortunate; they could control their direction.

A wind gusting above 20 miles per hour undermined the ability of others to navigate the current. An ever-growing stranded navy consisting ultimately of about 1500 floaters was driven across the river – and across an international boundary.

Not many had thought to bring along their passports or driver's licenses for this aquatic event. Some felt helpless to fight the current and yielded to their fate. Others, afraid of legal trouble if they were marooned in Canada, made feeble efforts to get away. Most were unsuccessful. They had succumbed to forces larger than themselves – the wind and the current.

Compressing the flowing waters of the largest lake in the world into a tiny funnel, the St. Clair River typically races southward. The current shoves an average 188,000 cubic feet per second of water downstream at a rate between 3 and 4 miles per hour. To put this into perspective, the infamous Chicago diversion drains Lake Michigan at a rate of no more than 3,200 cubic feet per second (a limit set by the courts). The St. Clair's roiling waters are evident, even a little alarming, to the casual observer.

In some areas of the world it would have been remarkable that authorities in a foreign nation provided concern, care and relatively swift bus service to return the refugees of the wind to their homeland. But however appreciated by the Float Down participants, the hospitality of the City of Sarnia, Ontario was typical of US. -Canadian boundary relations, even after September 11, 2001. Authorities imposed stricter requirements for boundary crossers but the transit was generally brisk.

The final cost of Sarnia's hospitality was $8,200. The Canadian Coast Guard estimated its contribution as approximately $22,000. On the U.S. side, St. Clair County and the City of Port Huron estimated $10,000. Sarnia officials generously refused to seek reimbursement from governments in the U.S., where Float Down originated.

"1,500 Americans showed up on our shores and we welcomed them," said Sarnia Mayor Mark Bradley. "It was extremely well handled by all the agencies involved on both sides of the border. We always try to entrap the American tourists in Sarnia, so why not do it the right way?"

On the other hand, Bradley warned about a narrow escape. "I'm hoping that some common sense will spring out of this. We could have had a major tragedy on our hands if the weather had been a bit more violent or the day had been a bit more wild on the river."

Embarrassed about the imposition on their Canadian neighbors, some Americans began Internet fundraising to pay them back.

Goodwill abounded – mostly. The shipping industry was even unhappier than before and called for the Float Down to be outlawed.

Chapter 15

Libby Harris was one of my earliest environmental mentors. I have never lived up to her model, but it's been worth trying. Thoughtful, principled and caring, she quietly reached out to me during a career crisis and I've never forgotten it.

She served as the executive director of the East Michigan Environmental Action Council after attending Tufts University, the University of Michigan and Wayne State University Law School in Detroit, where she acquired her law degree. Until I interviewed her for this book, I didn't know that she had worked as a VISTA volunteer, Michigan Supreme Court law clerk, attorney for Michigan Legal Assistance Services, and employee in a private law firm.

"My first memory of the Great Lakes," she said, "is a family vacation at Pentwater in the 1950's. I felt happy and safe there. My mental association with Lake Michigan is of my family together, playing on the beach, in the waves, fishing from the pier with long bamboo pools.

Having traveled the northern route from the Twin Cities to Michigan and back several times, I was struck by Libby's disclosure that when she drove west across the Upper Peninsula to Minnesota she stopped along US-2 west of St. Ignace to walk the Lake Michigan beach. I do the same. It's probably the most scenic roadway in America, and in any weather but driving snow stopping is irresistible. For several miles the federal road parallels the shore with unparalleled vistas of water and sky.

Libby said the Lakes are getting worse. Her list of menacing problems included invasive species and climate change—specifically, warming water temperatures that encourage algae blooms and reduced ice cover that threatens native species. "The toxic chemicals of concern in the 1970s have been reduced, but they haven't disappeared. And some, like mercury, are a concern again."

While she was aware of worrisome trends, her friends, Libby said, "talk about Great Lakes primarily in terms of summer vacations."

As is befitting of a former professional who was engaged in public policy, Libby had firm opinions about the role of government, and the pressures limiting it. She said EPA and state and provincial environmental agencies were collectively responsible for protecting the Lakes but without citizen expressions of support their capacity was limited.

"The will of the political party in power" accounted for much of the fluctuation in government treatment of the Lakes. Libby characterized the work of the two federal governments overall as mediocre. She had a slightly higher opinion of the performance of Great Lakes states and provinces.

Libby had told me her concern about the environment intensified after the chemical contamination of Michigan's food supply by the fire retardant PBB in 1973. A young mother at the time, she worried about the health of her two children. She didn't trust the state's current recommendations on safe consumption of Great Lakes fish by women of child bearing age. Instead of limiting consumption, "I think a safer approach for women who are pregnant, intending to become pregnant and those who are breastfeeding would be to avoid Great Lakes fish."

Libby's answer to my stock question about reasons for the struggles of the Lakes elicited a well-considered response. "They're deteriorating because individuals feel powerless to make a difference, because many of them assume governmental agencies have the power and responsibility to protect the Lakes, and because some only think about the Lakes when they're recreating on or near them."

As an example, Libby said, "This past August, the beach at Port Crescent State Park on Lake Huron was closed for swimming due to e. Coli. People were unhappy but only until the beach was reopened."

As always, Libby offered her opinions without rancor. But I sensed she was frustrated. Like me, she had spent a career trying to induce a better environment by empowering the public. Now we were hearing that some people thought of the Great Lakes only when dreaming of summer escapes. That people treasured them for leisure was reassuring, but it was distressing to recognize their thought processes stopped there.

Maybe a reason for the decline of the Great Lakes was that the advocacy strategies I had practiced simply didn't engage them.

Interlude 15

In our culture, a river is typically a boundary, differentiating one domain from another. The Mississippi River, for example, is the border of 10 states.

There's another way to look at a river – as the center of a basin, accepting and uniting all of its tributary waters. And its tributary people.

I've lived in several communities whose rivers and streams, acting like the solvent that water is, blurred or erased differences of age, ethnicity, and class. At certain times – say, summer evenings – these waters lured a cross-section of locals to trek their river walks, fish from their banks, boat or kayak their surface, or simply sit and enjoy their serene passage. No political tests were administered.

This is not a minor truth in an age of American division. As the right and left, the Republican and Democratic Parties, the environmentalists and the developers clash over almost everything – and often bitterly – I've seen quantitative and qualitative evidence that water washes away much of the antipathy. Water, in short, is something people of all kinds want to protect.

Nothing – not the division of human beings from the natural world, our tethering to gadgets, our exaltation of boundless economic growth – has dispelled our appreciation of water. Perhaps that's because water is one of the relatively few things in the natural world that comes to meet us in our homes. Thanks to modern drinking water delivery systems, the only invitation to enter that water needs is a twist of the faucet. And once it enters, it serves us in many ways. It is a hard heart that does not feel wonder, or at least gratitude, for this service – the magic of quenching our thirst, the mystery of dissolving stains.

Wonder also lives outdoors. Water makes music, carries us downstream, reflects light into art. Water doesn't distinguish among us by political philosophy. We all get its benefits.

A recent arrival in the Traverse region of Michigan, I don't know much about the community yet, so I'm observing and listening. I take comfort from my initial impressions. Philosophies of government span left to right here, but philosophies of water meet in the middle.

No one wants to watch our rivers and lakes deteriorate or dry up. Everyone here, it seems, enjoys those rivers and lakes, and makes use of them in one fashion or another. That gives me hope.

Another cause for hope is the absence of complacency. It would be understandable if this community took its water riches for granted. Even the most beautiful of environments can become a stale backdrop if it's present every day. I don't see that here.

The poets and musicians sing of it, the nonprofits educate and work to protect it – and especially when it comes to the Great Lakes, there is virtual unanimity about the need for stewardship.

Here's a good sign such universal protectiveness exists. Focus groups of Trump voters in the Great Lakes region agreed that water is the most precious resource, universally ranking above other environmental concerns. In one group, water quality and water pollution were the top-rated environmental problems.

We can do better. And we will. The affinity we feel for water is the foundation for learning.

Chapter 16

At 34, Sarah Clement had analyzed the environment – and seen the world – in ways that surpassed anything I had done with an extra 25 years. At the time she answered my questions, Dr. Clement, as I never called her, was teaching at the University of Liverpool.

She had impressed me when she worked briefly at the Michigan Environmental Council in 2003. We had intermittently corresponded in subsequent years. Until she mentioned coming home to visit family in 2016, I had had no idea that she had spent much of her youth in the Port Huron area.

Sarah was more than a theoretician. She had worked for an environmental consulting firm, sampling soil and water, surveying wetlands and studying groundwater. Only subsequently had she gone on to study environmental policy, management and governance.

She said one of her first Great Lakes memories was of Pentwater Beach on Lake Michigan.

"We used to sometimes travel from our cottage on a little lake near Clare to Pentwater for the day. I remember feeling like I was at the ocean in California, with the beautiful white sand and all the people on the crowded beach. Then I got in the water, and it was so incredibly cold that I knew for sure I was in Michigan. My siblings and I used to compete to see who could stay in the icy water for the longest. I always lost."

On her visit in the summer of 2016, Sarah went to Lakeside Beach near Port Huron with her family. "It wasn't quite as cold as those memories of Pentwater, but it was certainly rockier," she said. "I remember wishing I had brought my water shoes and laughing because my Australian husband had never heard of such a thing. That part of the lake is really rocky under foot. I collected rocks with my niece and laughed at my dad who stood on the beach on a 90-degree day in a t-shirt, jeans, socks, and tennis shoes."

. She said something close to how I had felt for years. "I feel sentimental about Lake Michigan, in awe of Superior, nostalgic for my teenage years when I see Lake Huron, and concerned about Lake Erie. I actually think I appreciate them more now that I have moved away and travelled quite a lot."

Viewing the Great Lakes through the scientist's lens, Sarah called it very important to protect them not just "because I believe in the intrinsic value of the lakes, which I do, but also because they provide essential ecosystem services to people both within and outside the region."

Her view of the state of the Lakes was colored by her reading of journal articles and reports, which are about investigating problems and testing hypotheses. Based on that data she said she felt the Lakes were worsening. "I'll occasionally read a good bit of news, for example about recovery of sturgeon, but I seem to see so much more on nutrient pollution, unsustainable water withdrawals, declines of fish stocks, and increases in non-native species. I'm heartened by the quality of the research that is going on in the region, but disheartened by the lack of influence that research has on policy and action."

She had studied and analyzed land issues in Australia and brought that into our discussion. She cited "poor land management" as the top threat to the Great Lakes. "It's such a broad scale problem that is more complex and challenging to address with policy interventions than point sources, but doing so is essential to improving water quality in the lakes."

Who's in charge of the Great Lakes?

"That's a very complex question with no clear answer. There are a lot of different organizations with responsibility for managing and protecting the lakes, and then many other organizations and individuals with responsibility for activities that influence the health of the lakes. I guess I would say that, from a statutory perspective, it's probably the environmental agencies in each state. However, the International Joint Commission has a crucial role as an independent advisory body with a holistic view of the Great Lakes, even if their recommendations are non-binding."

Individuals make a difference in protecting the quality of the Great Lakes, Sarah said, such as changing purchasing and consumption decisions and lawn care practices. Advocacy with politicians and officeholders was important. But the political scientist said "it cannot be a replacement for institutional change if we really want to see the lakes improve."

The election to the Presidency of Donald Trump had flipped her from optimism. "Climate change is one of the greatest challenges for the lakes and the environment in general, and I'm fairly certain little will be done in this arena for the next 4-8 years. We are about to have a president that wants to dismantle the EPA and believes climate change is a Chinese conspiracy. He also has this antiquated notion that you can either have a strong economy or a healthy environment, but not both. I had hoped we were past that now."

"There are many murmurings that we are living in a 'post-truth' era, and from where I sit, this certainly seems to ring true. The lakes need strong, science-based policy and management if they are to improve. I'm not so sure we are living in a time when that can happen."

Her thoughts on the gap between public sentiment and the health of the Lakes were a wealth of possibilities. The scientific literature, she said, offered explanations for why people don't always act consistently with their emotions or belief.

"Do people really feel like they can individually act to help the lakes? Do they feel they can act autonomously and effectively? They probably feel like it's out of their control. There's also a connection between intention and action: do people intend to perform the actions that favor a healthier Great Lakes system? Do they have the knowledge and resources to do so?" she asked.

Perhaps the Great Lakes don't rank highly relative to other preferences or needs, she suggested. "Maybe caring for the lakes is a strong social norm that people feel they should express in surveys, but that they ultimately do not hold very strongly themselves," Sarah said. "Maybe it's just the same as so many other behaviors. We all know we should eat more vegetables, exercise, and drive less, but most of us don't do these things."

These science-driven explanations made me uncomfortable, not because they were inaccurate, but because they suddenly seemed quite accurate. My experiences were consistent with some of these hypotheses. I didn't want to believe them. If true, they might mean the lakes were doomed.

But Sarah wasn't giving up. Why should I?

When I asked her to sum up her feelings about the Great Lakes in one sentence, the scholar spoke. "I feel the Great Lakes are remarkable and unique resources that are underappreciated outside of the region." When I asked her to summarize her feelings in one word, her heart spoke: "precious."

Interlude 16

Are the Great Lakes getting better or worse?

Any good scientist will tell you that's a short question with a long answer, a simple question with a complicated answer. And after a half hour of trying to explain it to you, they will have made it only a little simpler. If you're lucky.

So why is it so difficult to create a report card informing the interested public about the condition of the Great Lakes?

It's not that people haven't been trying. Beginning in the 1990s, the many talented Great Lakes scientists and government agency staff presented data on so-called indicators at State of the Lake Ecosystem Conference (SOLEC) gatherings. They offered up scores of measures including the health of benthic organisms, levels of chemical contaminants in herring gull eggs, the number of public beach closings, the quality of finished drinking water, phosphorus concentrations in water, toxic air pollutants deposited to water, and more. Each indicator had a rationale, and most had solid data to back them up.

But there were too many – over 100 at the beginning, and approximately 80 as late as 2011. The array of likely and potential indicators was so large that it constituted an unfathomable Great Lakes report card. How to simplify?

While the scientists wrestled with their data and discussed which indicators best told the story of Great Lakes health, taxpayers spent hundreds of millions of U.S. and Canadian dollars without lucid measures of whether they were paying for improvement. Pressure was building. And something happened.

Following the 2011 SOLEC, organizers created a highlights report to distill what the indicators said. Organized around the three principal results sought by governments --protection of the physical, chemical and biological integrity of the Great Lakes ecosystem – the report contained a clear verdict -— to a point:

Water quality status is fair and the trend is deteriorating.

Aquatic-dependent life status is fair and the trend is deteriorating.

Landscapes and natural processes status is fair and the trend is improving.

Two out of three indicator groupings deteriorating? No rocket scientists were needed to explain that one. But "aquatic-dependent life" is a term not many members of the public could define.

The highlights report put it this way: "The overall deteriorating trend for aquatic-dependent life is a result of decreasing preyfish populations, the declining population of Diporeia (a source of food for small fish), and the declining populations of many coastal wetland species. The food web has been drastically altered."

As the statement suggests, judgments about a profoundly complex natural system are themselves complicated. They address matters and species that generalists never consider. It's no wonder that the experts have resisted simplifying the ecosystem to an A through E elementary school style report card.

Although publicly available, the data and conclusions in the highlights report were not widely broadcast. You had to look for them on the Internet.

It was still not a report card, but governments and scientists were getting there.

The International Joint Commission devoted considerable time and some money to prodding the Canadian and U.S. governments to narrow the list, recommending 16 indicators – but 41 "measures." One recommended indicator was persistent, bioaccumulative toxins in biota, but consisted of two measures, chemicals in whole fish and chemicals in herring gull eggs and bald eagles. It was a step toward simplification, but it demonstrated that even when bringing the number of indicators down, governments and scientists would and perhaps could go only so far.

A report card was still important. Without it, the public would be left to draw conclusions based on hunches, anecdotes or a misleading façade. For example, clearer water means healthier water, right? Not necessarily. Invasive zebra mussels, by consuming plankton in the water column, clarified it, but no one seriously argued that invasive mussels were a good thing. The plankton they consumed would ordinarily have fed native prey fish.

The report card effort, like almost everything else bearing on the health of the Great Lakes, pivots on how much work citizens are willing – or able -- to do in understanding the waters they love. They must meet the scientists halfway.

They do not need to know the details of even 20 indicators, but they need to know one, two or three examples so they grasp the way these pieces fit into a large puzzle.

They do not need to use the term "aquatic dependent life," but they need to understand the concept of an aquatic food web and its importance.

They do not need to recognize physical, chemical and biological integrity, but they do need to understand the analogous values of swimmable, fishable and drinkable waters.

They do not need to go to the Internet to find a SOLEC highlights report, but they do need to insist that the governments develop something akin to a report card – and then they need to do something with the results.

Chapter 17

Judge Derwin Rushing. Those are three words I would not have expected to be joined when I met Derwin in 1975. Oh, he was smart enough, but I thought him an only semi-attentive business major and, with a quick sense of humor, too light-hearted for the job of facing down lawbreakers.

I revised my opinion of him within a few months as he educated me on nuclear energy, gun control and civil liberties. Thinking myself more informed than the typical citizen, I was humbled by his superior knowledge.

Then, as his housemate while he attended law school in the early 1980s, I watched in stunned amazement as he studied and attended class 50 hours a week for three years. He wanted that law degree with all his soul. We remained friends over the decades as he married Darlene and as they later moved to Pittsburgh. It was heartening when he won election as a Magisterial District Judge in the Fifth Judicial District of Pennsylvania, Allegheny County. His idealism was untainted. He made a first-class jurist.

Born in 1954, Derwin grew up in a working-class neighborhood in a suburb south of Detroit, the son of a blue collar worker.

"Unfortunately," he said, "my first memory of being on a Great Lake was not a good one. One sunny afternoon before I was old enough to be in school, my Mom and our neighbor Mrs. Risner decided go to Lake Erie for the day someplace near Monroe. The beach wasn't crowded, there were people, three and four here and there and none in the water. Large signs posted in the sand every fifty feet explained that some contaminant in the lake had made it dangerous to swim. I could wade in the sand near the shore, but I couldn't let the water touch me and so like everyone else we left."

He and Darlene had encouraged me to rent the Lake Huron cottage just 500 feet from their own, sharing the bounty. Their connection to the Port Huron-Lexington area reached back to the 1980s, before they met in a community theater company. During that time Derwin and his cousin had twisted my arm into joining them in one of the early float downs on the St. Clair River.

"I can see the lake through a space between the trees of my neighbor's house across the street. I spend as much of the summer there as I can," he said.

He remarked on the lake's power. "I have seen shingles ripped from roofs in straight rows and sent rapid fire. And at other times the lake is as placid as a Buddha in prayer."

An astute observer and avocational writer, he wanted to read from one of his pieces. I told him to go ahead.

"At eight pounds a gallon and eight hundred and fifty cubic miles, Lake Huron is heavy. Were she suddenly lifted from the globe, the planet would wobble. Every body of water is always a woman. Always the same by being always different. A fury, to be avoided, that is new each time and a beauty that defies the most tortured of poets. And, affected by moon-tides. And, just like water, you can't possibly live without out her but for a short time and to taste her is to slack thirst that is its own reward."

Just 40 miles from Lake Michigan when we were students at Western Michigan University, Derwin had spent considerable time on that lake for a few years, but had since been largely Huron's companion. Friends from the Port Huron community were conversant about their lake's condition, but those in Pittsburgh, 90 miles from Lake Erie, were "woefully ignorant" of Huron and shocked to learn of its size.

Lake Huron was a palpable presence in Darlene and Derwin's cottage, which she had decorated in part with a nautical theme. Shipwrecks and lighthouses were among the artifacts.

Like most whom I interviewed, Derwin thought it crucial to protect the Lakes. In a time of rapidly rising demand for fresh water, a failure to protect the Lakes would lead to a global catastrophe, he said.

He offered some more writing: "It's a reflection of our spirit as a species that we live within the wise administration of our resources or we die wallowing in our own filth, giving proof to a theory positing that the human animal is a filthy animal and as character is destiny, one day we will simply poison the well."

By his "totally unscientific observation," he said, the Great Lakes are at least holding their own if not getting better. In Pittsburgh the rivers were growing cleaner and biological diversity increasing, so it would stand to reason, he said, that the nearby Lakes are at least staying the same.

After listing several commonly mentioned issues, he said, "I think above them all the number one threat is the lack of political will to address current problems and plan for the near, and distant, future. The lack of will to act as responsible stewards in our trust of the Lakes."

A public official himself, and active politically all his adult life, Derwin said influence was easily accomplished.

"A simple call to your appropriate representative has enormous impact, more than people realize, particularly on this issue because it generally isn't number one on anyone's radar so any interest that is shown is magnified," he observed.

Derwin retained an optimism that was all the more compelling given his awareness, seasoned with wry humor, of human imperfection.

"Ultimately, I'm hopeful for the Lakes. I'm hopeful for them because the younger generation gives me hope, in the degree and breadth of their commitment to a belief system that assumes greater balance with the natural world."

I wasn't going to dispute that.

Interlude 17

Winter played tag the second time around. At the end of January only two minor snowstorms had struck. More often than not, I could walk my dog up and down the beach. And I finally learned to listen, a little.

On days of light wind, the lake still generated tiny waves. Reaching the shore, they washed over the mash of pebbles, making a fizzing sound like an uncapped soda. It was a subtle thing that I had ignored scores of times before.

The lake still roared or groaned many days and nights. For a while, even when the temperature plunged below the freezing point, Huron seethed.

I was gone one night on business and when I returned, I noticed an absence. The lake was mute. I walked down to the beach. A thin glaze capped the waters. All curves and angles less than 48 hours before, the lake was now flat, and silent. Even though it was natural, it was unnerving; as if someone had forbidden the lake to speak.

A few days later, the temperature moderated and the lake burst from its shackles of ice. It was extraordinary. I walked down to the beach on the few days of January with adequate supplies of sunlight and, with careful framing, captured photographs that resembled summer scenes.

On January 26, almost a month after the closing of the St. Lawrence Seaway, my photographs displayed the profile of a freighter. According to marinetraffic.com, it was the 43-year-old Manitowoc, apparently awaiting an errand in Sarnia, for it was anchored several miles out. It seemed remarkable that a vessel like the Manitowoc was still doing business as we neared the halfway point of winter. But on January 27 the Algosteel cruised past, ultimately reaching Goderich, Ontario.

On one of the rare two-day spells of temperatures below freezing, my brother and I walked Fitz beside the St. Clair River just south of the Bluewater Bridge. The wind stung our faces and flung tiny snow pellets at us. The river was chewing on ice. That's how it sounded as patches of it proceeded downriver hurriedly, colliding and clashing. The peculiar part of my mind thought of each large fragment of ice as a being, jockeying for space to breathe as it moved downstream. That line of thinking would ultimately lead to the death of the ice beings and thoughts of death in general, so I engaged my brother in conversation.

Even a mild winter can feel forbidding at times. The silence of the nearly abandoned cottage colony and the view of the typically unoccupied gray mat of water from my landlord's patio fed a sense of desolation. The memory of summer afternoons when the same view revealed countless sailboats, power boats, and a few kayaks and freighters was haunting.

The creek – actually a county drain – that slithered lazily to the south of my cottage, almost dying out before it reached the lake, suddenly exploded in an overnight January rainstorm. When I walked down to examine it, I saw it had knifed through a three-foot layer of sand built up by the windstorms of fall. It took a leap, not a step, to cross it; I had to pick up Fitz to bring him along on our walk. He refused to make the jump on his own.

A progression of sunless days suppressed my appreciation of Huron. On some I spent only a few minutes by the lake, impatiently awaiting Fitz's bowel movements, and hurrying him and me back to the warmth of the indoors. It was disappointing that I could come to take living by the lake for granted. But it was human.

And then one late afternoon a high wind tore the cloud cover into pieces, and as the sun set, it illuminated the under belly of the clouds over the lake a soft purple. I was back in love – a quiet and undemonstrative love that was sinking roots like other surviving transplants.

Chapter 18

I met Maureen Martin when she was a fundraiser on the staff of The Nature Conservancy. Over the years, as she continued to excel in winning funds for good institutions, Maureen revealed a gentle yet earthy streak and an uproarious sense of humor. She also demonstrated a deep bond with Michigan's outdoors.

About six months younger than me, Maureen (or Mo, as her partner Mike Penskar called her) was another Detroit area baby and had lived in Michigan all but three years of her life.

Her career had initially been a zigzag – work at restaurants and bars during college, journalist at a weekly paper, and indexing newspapers. Then she organized her life, going to night school and business school. She found her niche as a successful fundraiser for nonprofit theater (in Oregon and New York City), education reform, conservation, a museum/charter school and finally the University of Michigan.

"Probably my two earliest Great Lakes memories are of the dunes of Lake Michigan," she said. "In one, I'm very small and at Sleeping Bear Dunes. I remember the souvenir black bear more than the dunes, and the feeling of running down the dunes with my brothers. The second early memory is of boating across Silver Lake to the dunes there, and walking across those dunes to Lake Michigan, looking for what we called the Lost City buried in the dunes. "

Maureen's family life featured summer camping trips to the state parks of Michigan – Copper Harbor, Ludington, Silver Lake, Wilderness, Indian River – that involved three generations of aunts, uncles, grandparents, parents, and siblings. "These trips were full of love and belonging and laughter," she remembered fondly. "We swam, water skied, collected rocks, walked the shore. My father and grandmother were patient anglers who would stay out on boats for the days then cook up dinner and play cards for the evenings."

She turned lyrical. "The lakes open up my heart. They make me feel a part of the physical universe – like a biological animal who found her way to water. Swimming in them makes me feel seven years old, especially if there are waves for body surfing.

"I love the beach house at Ludington State Park – it's a part of my story for nearly all of my 59 years. I know the campsites we stayed at in Cedars campground when I was little, Aunt Barb over there, Grandma on that one with Grampa Ted; I know where we were at Beechwood a different year. And in the Pines with my aunt Millie and uncle Bob and cousins on my Mom's side (the other side from Aunt Barb and Grandma). I know the Pines sites where my generation rekindled the summer trips when the first grandkids showed up. Some years it seems like those sites look like refugee camps, smoke and trucks and tents crowding the park. But it doesn't matter. We laughed and drank and were nearly evicted for after-hours noise on many occasions, and we embarrassed my mom no end with our rowdiness. We played Ditch on the dunes as teens. We hid from rangers on ATVs in the late night hours."

Maureen wasn't an armchair steward of the Lakes. "I've kayaked in Lake Michigan on day trips (sea kayaks rented or borrowed). I also had the great adventure of a multi-day trip kayaking the Apostle Islands in Lake Superior – what an incredible time. There's such wonder in those five-foot swells and such relief to make land on Devil's Island and such joy when the big crossing, five miles from the nearest Island, I think, was completed."

Lake Michigan had wooed and won many of those I interviewed, including Maureen. "I love Lake Michigan into my DNA. If I had all the money in the world, it's Lake Michigan I would want to live with. The sandy shores and the winds and the sunsets all bring me to my knees. I admire Lake Superior in its unwillingness to be tamed, but its shores are for sturdier souls than me."

Having worked for TNC, she had links to many conservationists who obsessed about policies and talked about them.

"But when I'm with friends and talk turns to the Lakes, it's usually about getting out on them on boats – kayaks, freighters. Or visiting one of the shoreline towns. I'm not sure we very often focus on policy – maybe passing references – since it's a given we're all on the same side and are engaged in our ways. Maybe a collective rolling of the eyes about Nestle. Or Asian carp."

Her one sentence about the Lakes: "I am 'of this place' – the waters of the Great Lakes define my place in this world and when they're out of reach, my eyes ache for the blue waters, big pines and green deciduous trees." One word: "Belonging."

She had concerns. "The Great Lakes are being redefined/rebuilt. The fisheries are changed in ways that likely cannot be undone. I suppose, ecologically, I would say they are getting worse – the loss of the underwater ecosystem is near-total, I think. I'd love us to contemplate what 'restoration' might look like – and, I suppose, to what era would we restore? My dad was a salmon fisherman – and salmon is gone from Lake Huron, as an example. I say that, knowing that salmon was an introduced species."

Her optimism was of a kind common to environmentally concerned people I know. "I believe the lakes will outlive us humans," she said, "and that they'll evolve to recover from our presence. I suppose that's a hopeful reading."

She wrote out a list of causes for the declining health of the Lakes: "Distributed responsibility. Long term investment needed; faith; sacrifice – not things we humans are very good at – either in politics or other spheres."

More interested in envisioning an ideal future for the Great Lakes, she said "'better' is not, to me, compelling. I want to picture – what's the best-case scenario for these waters and what would it take to get us there? Shovel-ready Superfund sites is just not my idea of a worthy vision for restoration," she said.

"How many years, how much work, by whom, would it take to restore health and vitality to the system? I wonder if a tribal strategy might not be optimal? That is – tribal rights as a binational driver toward restoration and access? I'm a bit exhausted with our compromise position that draws on economy and resource extraction as the drivers of political will. I want our fantasy to be built on ecology and well-being more than practical uses. Our lifelong compromises have trained us to bargain downward to salmon fisheries and docks instead of focusing on ecology and wonder."

She took another turn and mused on something that had vexed me. What would we do if water scarcity caused a humanitarian crisis somewhere? Would we deny Great Lakes water to save lives? "How is it that an accident of geography – where we were born, say, or where we choose to live – determines that it is our water to live by and isn't meant to be shared with others?"

"But that is a doomsday idea predicated on there being a global freshwater shortage."

We both knew that was coming. It was only a question of when.

Interlude 18

Science has told us much about the Great Lakes, and it has told us little when compared to what we need.

Suppose that around the year 2030, global population and global climate change collide in a potentially catastrophic water shortage. After deliberation and in the face of some organized opposition, the President, Congress and the Great Lakes states agree with the Canadian government to authorize emergency shipments in oceangoing vessels of Great Lakes water to hard hit regions of the developing world. How much? Well, no one's sure. The first priority is to start the shipments to save lives while scientists assist policymakers in determining at what point the exports will damage the Great Lakes. Then it will be up to the policymakers to decide how much damage is acceptable.

A fundamental problem is that there is no identifiable point at which an unnaturally lowered water level of one or all of the Great Lakes results in damage. The four lower Lakes have natural fluctuations of between six and seven feet. And the Lakes are so great in volume that even a large withdrawal lowers them relatively little. Diverting enough water to supply 7 million people in Illinois has lowered the level of Lake Michigan-Huron between two and three inches. Seven million Americans use much more water than seven million people in the developing world. Is another two or three inches such a big deal?

And yet there are scientists and lake advocates that remind us there is no surplus water in the Great Lakes. Each drop serves a purpose, finds its place in the grand Great Lakes, and grand global ecosystems. Moving those drops in untold numbers will have uncertain effects but is sure to have an effect. Science can give us knowledgeable guidance, but no simple answers.

So what do we do?

The Great Lakes Compact among the eight Great Lakes States and the parallel agreement that also includes Ontario and Quebec provide an exception to the partial ban on diversions for short-term humanitarian purposes (as well as firefighting and emergency response). "Short-term" and "humanitarian" are not defined. The jurisdictions will have to cobble definitions together as they go. Or perhaps the extent of the calamity will make abstractions like these definitions moot.

The imperative of saving human lives will be paramount. But when I think of what happens to the Great Lakes under such circumstances, I'm reminded of the children's book The Giving Tree *by Shel Silverstein. The story traces the relationship between a tree and a boy who spends happy hours of youth swinging from it and enjoying its apples. But in the prime of manhood he comes to the tree only to satisfy material wants. The tree yields up revenue from the sale of its apples and wood for a house and a boat. Finally, in its old age, the Giving Tree is nothing but a stump. The boy, turned old man, comes back to his beloved tree and uses what is left the only way he can – as a place to sit and rest. He's still using.*

We can't let the Great Lakes become the aquatic equivalent of a stump.

Chapter 19

For years, driving from my office at the Michigan Environmental Council in Lansing to a meeting at the Ecology Center in Ann Arbor was a mini-vacation. We did good work, and usually hard work together, but more important to me was being among kindred spirits who poured their passion into protecting environmental health.

One of them was Tracey Easthope. Specializing in chemical policy, she was a walking website who could answer almost any question on the subject – and many others. She was the Michigan environmental community's prime resource on public health. She was also nationally recognized, serving on the advisory board of a journal of environmental and occupational health theory.

She was quietly fierce about her work but a thoughtful, sensitive friend. My chief worry about her was that she gave so much of herself to her advocacy. How much did she save for enjoying life? I was honored that she took the time to answer my questions.

Yet another product of a Detroit hospital, Tracey was 56 when we connected about this. She'd lived in the Ann Arbor area for approximately the prior 53 years. Her degrees were from schools within the general area, including a master's in public health from the University of Michigan and, more recently a bachelor's in fine arts from Eastern Michigan University. She was cultivating her gift as a sculptor now, while still promoting sane chemical policy. For one exhibit in Saugatuck, she offered the statement, "I am interested in using materials in my sculptures that humans have been working with for generations." Her life and work are interconnected.

I wasn't surprised that she had a vivid, early Great Lakes memory. "I'm not sure if I remember the day or the photograph, but in the photo, my lovely mother and I are standing on a sandy beach with small white rocks like little dragees on sheet cake," she wrote. "There's a particular blue color you see in the sky and lake on a cold sunny day that is so stunning. I am maybe 3 or 4, bending down examining a rock, and my bright white hair swirls around my head and completely covers my face. My Mom stands next to me holding my hand, while keeping her coat closed against the wind– I think we are at Lake Superior. I don't know when I understood that knowing the Lakes was enough in a life, but it must have started early."

Her treasury of Great Lakes memories wasn't all benign. Vacationing on Lake Huron when she was 10, Tracey said, she was caught by a powerful wave "that held me under water for a long time. Frightened and alone, I remember the panic and the flailing – and then, the calm. The peacefulness was so surprising before the wave let go."

Her recent Great Lakes memory replicated one that I now enjoyed several times a week – and her mention of it reminded me not to take it for granted. Just before Christmas of 2016 "we went to visit my partner's parents, who live in a neighborhood next to Lake Michigan. We arrived after dark on a windy night and opened the car door to a noise like some beast roaring – no rhythm like a tide, just a sustained roar. And later, at Hoffmaster State Park, we hiked through the snowy woods midday to the shore to see the beast – gray in the daylight with big peaks of frothy spittle. It was too cold to stay long but we had paid our respects."

Protecting the Great Lakes, she said, "is the most important thing we can do as Michiganders, after protecting each other, although the two are linked. As a colleague says, you can't have healthy people on a sick planet, and you can't have healthy Michiganders if the Lakes are sick." As for the condition of the aquatic patient, she thought it mixed. Old banned chemicals, for example, were in decline while new nasties were being detected in fish and wildlife.

Also more complex than a one-word answer was the choice of the leading threat to the Great Lakes. Tracey was too intelligent to come out with even a one-liner.

"I would guess a combination of threats – global warming, loss of wetlands, toxic threats, invasive species, development – has made the Lakes less resilient to any additional assault. So the loss of resilience is now the big threat -- we have eliminated any margin of safety --- so any additional or increasing threat greatly imperils the Lakes," she said.

What could an individual do to protect the Lakes? "The list is long but several categories come to mind, including loving and experiencing the Lakes -- this is critical -- making art related to the Lakes, changing personal behaviors to protect the Lakes, advocating for the Lakes."

I was curious whether my peer heard any political talk among her friends or colleagues about the Lakes. "That's an interesting question," she said. "I don't think they talk much about saving them, strangely. We talk together endlessly about enjoying them, and experiencing them, and being near them." I thought that might be good, especially given her thought about the need to get out and savor the Lakes.

Then came the most sweeping diagnosis anyone had made about the reasons for the struggles of the Lakes in the face of public adoration:
"It's probably a mixture of things." She cited:
- A "terrible, abominable, outrageous lack of leadership in Michigan" that failed to acknowledge the issues or to call citizens to be part of the protection of the Lakes;
- powerful industry interests bent on reducing regulations and costs
- an indifferent federal government
- a long-term reduction in resources devoted to studying and understanding the lakes

- the collapse of an environmental beat in journalism and local news coverage
- long term disinvestment in infrastructure
- people's failure to connect their actions with the health of the lakes
- a consumer culture that values convenience and acquisitiveness
- the phenomenon of the tragedy of the commons
- rapacious developers
- long range global transport of pollutants
- sharing a resource with two different nations
- the modern Republican Party's hostility to science and to natural resources
- ineffectual Democrats
- the erosion of democracy in general
- economic insecurity, "and insecure people must first focus on surviving, making it more difficult to engage them in Great Lakes protection."

She concluded: "I don't really know." But she had just shown me she did.

Tracey added that about the future of the lakes, she couldn't bear to say anything except that she was hopeful. Polling suggested Michiganders had a unique and abiding connection to the Lakes, she said. "I think we love the Lakes enough that we should be able to save them."

I wasn't surprised that Tracey had refused to simplify things. She didn't tailor her words or thoughts to what was expected. To do so would be to patronize. Tracey was as far from that as you can get. In addition to an impressive mind, she had absolute integrity.

Interlude 19

What do you do when your hosts are making every effort to anticipate your needs but they unintentionally test your principles? The correct action isn't always easy to determine.

When writing the biography of Michigan's longest-serving governor, William Milliken, I visited the Traverse City house he and his wife Helen owned on the west arm of Grand Traverse Bay to conduct interviews. Helen, a major public figure in her own right, offered to make lunch. When the three of us sat down to eat, I was staring in the face of a BLT – and I was a vegetarian. I spent a few seconds wondering whether I should advise the Millikens of my dining preferences or just eat the BLT. I ate it and said nothing. I was fortunate to be served anything by these two elegant people.

I've probably given a hundred speeches or more over the years, generally at the invitation of friendly organizations interested in filling a half hour or an hour with information about environmental issues. In recent years, I'll get to the podium to find a plastic bottle of water ready to lubricate my words.

My first impulse is to flinch. Because by the time I notice the bottle, I am about to speak to an audience, I can't privately ask the bottle be removed. My second impulse is to ponder whether I should make a point in my presentation about the bottle. But I don't. It's bad manners.

But we need a different set of norms, one in which serving what belongs to the public – water – that is captured by private parties and packaged at an enormous markup in price is considered bad form. Bottled water sold by private parties is a sneak attack on the Great Lakes and other public waters.

These parties, including large multinational companies, have the resources to package their arguments in pretty containers just like the water. They're good for communities, they say, because they create jobs. And the water they take is privately owned. After all, they pump it on private property.

That last argument sounds convincing to some on first hearing, but it's based on antiquated law and understanding of the hydrological cycle. When somebody pumps water from an aquifer that feeds a creek that feeds a river that feeds the Great Lakes, the Lakes are diminished, however imperceptibly. In law, however, the diminution is much larger. The authorities have determined that private parties can sell something that belongs to the people. Once that decision has been made, government, the trustee of the public interest, has lost control of water ownership.

Courts have clearly defined government's role as steward of common resources like water. A Michigan court has called it "a high, solemn and perpetual trust, which it is the duty of the state to forever maintain."

This is not a view all environmental groups share. Regulating the inevitable might best sum up their policy. Legislating standards companies taking water must follow to protect everything from groundwater flow to fish populations is more sensible than fighting the public ownership issue, in their view.

This is the latest front in the identity crisis in the environmental movement. It's as old as the movement itself. Is it better to negotiate, mitigate and regulate or to hold fast to major principles? The factions can make strong arguments for each side. But in the case of water, something is different.

To say that water is life is to affirm the obvious. None of us can live long without it. But a characteristic of water is what distinguishes it: flow. Water is naturally restless. It moves. That's why it's a natural highway, useful for humans. It's also a reason why it should not be owned.

If a company that is pumping Great Lakes tributary jabbed its pipe into Lake Michigan and took the exact amount it is instead taking from well upstream, the public outcry would be formidable. The popular imagination understands that Lake Michigan can't be owned. Yet Lake Michigan would be a dwarf without its tributaries. The difference is insubstantial in the physical world, and it should be in the world of policy and law.

If the Great Lakes community and others organized around protection of freshwater resources do not see that this is so – and if it's not too late already – the most precious substance we know is in danger of being controlled by private parties who exalt profit over protection. Will we have to pay them not to extract too much water for sale? Do we even have the funds to satisfy their greed?

In The Living Great Lakes: Searching for the Heart of the Inland Seas, *author Jerry Dennis wrote, "To appreciate the magnitude of the Great Lakes you must get close to them. Launch a boat on their waters or hike their beaches or climb the dunes, bluffs, and rocky promontories that surround them and you will see, as people have seen since the age of glaciers, that these lakes are pretty damned big. It's no wonder they're sometimes upgraded to 'Inland Seas' and 'Sweetwater Seas.' Calling them lakes is like calling the Rockies hills." The question is whether we will allow the Great Lakes to subside to hills.*

And that's why I will be openly refusing bottled water at any future speaking engagements. Besides, tap water tastes better.

Chapter 20

Many people have tried to capture the Great Lakes through photography, but no one has done it as well as Ed Wargin. "Photography" does not accurately describe his work. He makes his photographs on film, resulting in an exquisite, exhaustively prepared and executed art. It is *not* smartphone photography, which has incubated a false sense of artistry in many, well, including me at times.

I had a chance to write a foreword for a digital book of Ed's Great Lakes film photographs, and he made me look good. I sent the link to dozens of friends and received back the electronic equivalent of gasps of wonder.

You might infer from the first paragraph that Ed is wholly dedicated to his craft, and you'd be right. Another way of looking at it is that he has standards. I expected unadulterated views from him, and I got them.

Born in Duluth, Ed was 53 years old at the time of the interview. This far western end of the Great Lakes Basin was where Ed went to high school (Hermantown) and college (the University of Minnesota-Duluth). His formal resume included these job titles:

Narrative Fine Art Photographer, Editorial Creative Director, Editorial Photographer, Commercial Photographer, Photojournalist, Fine Art Darkroom Printer, Photo-Assistant, Producer, Grip, Studio Lighting Specialist, Print and Digital Publisher.

"My father worked in the Port of Duluth at the grain elevators, my oldest brother worked as a welder in the shipyards in Superior, Wisconsin for a time and my Finnish grandfather worked on the freighters and in various lumber camps along the north shore, so my memories of being connected to the lake run deep and generationally," Ed said. When I asked for a childhood memory, he invoked a drive up Minnesota's North Shore, a genuinely majestic landscape.

"It was inspiring, it was my first real glimpse of the sheer magnitude and size of Lake Superior. As we inched our way towards the Canadian border, I recall the large hills that comprise the landscape of the surrounding Thunder Bay area. It felt otherworldly and it still does to this day."

Only months before answering my questions, he had had an experience he remembered vividly. It was the first snowstorm of the season in October at Pictured Rocks National Lakeshore.

"All the leaves were in full color," Ed said. "The lighthouse on Grand Island was mostly obscured by the storm as I made my way through Munising. I eventually made my way to Chapel Rock. I attempted to make photographs there, but the icy snow pellets came right off the lake, up the sheer cliffs and pelted my lens and my face. It gave the appearance of being a vertical snowstorm."

Ed had an acquaintance with *his* lake like mine with Huron. "I see Lake Superior almost every single day from our living room window. The view is always a perfect indicator of the day's weather. I think I'd be at a loss if couldn't see the lake every single day," he said.

He was one of the few I interviewed who was actively enjoying a book related to the Great Lakes -- *Knife Island – Circling a Year in a Herring Skiff* by Stephen Dahl. It is told from the point of view of a commercial herring fisherman along Minnesota's North Shore of Lake Superior, done in a journal style, from season to season.

Ed's pride was evident when he discussed his current project, scanning his archival color reversal film library from 30 years of film projects on the Great Lakes. "When complete," he said, "it will be one of the most artistically comprehensive fine art narrative film libraries on the Great Lakes, by one sole artist. It holds an extensive cross section of works containing not just the landscapes and shorelines, but also the archival film collection holds unique imagery from certain locations that are seldom ever seen by the public such as Aldo Leopold's summer cottage in the Les Cheneaux Islands, [Michigan Supreme Court Justice and best-selling author] John Voelker's private fish camp in northern Michigan and numerous other locals throughout the Great Lakes. It's called The Great Lakes Film Collection.

Ed's one sentence about the Lakes: "With seemingly endless coasts, they will visually surrender to the wanderer only what it wants revealed." His one word: "Inimitable."

But he is concerned. "When you travel the Great Lakes as much I do, you often feel as if they're barely stabilized. I still continue to see evidence of pollution on almost every outing."

Why was this happening? He was blunt. "It is profound how much human pollution I see while working along the Great Lakes. I believe there's a growing disregard and lack of stewardship by citizens. If someone visits a beach, for example, and they're unwilling to bring their refuse to a garbage can —whether it's a simple water bottle or a plastic bag or a used diaper—then how will those people be advocates for the bigger issues the Great Lakes are facing? It's puzzling."

Ed thought it unfair that government was often the scapegoat for some of the problems of the Great Lakes, "I think responsibility must also fall on the citizens of the basin and beyond, if there's to be any hope for protecting and preserving the Great Lakes. I think people need to realize that the lakes might look like oceans, but they are not oceans. They are lakes and they can only handle so much abuse. It is NOT an infinite resource."

Many citizens were falling short of their stewardship responsibilities, he said. "As I see it from my work in the Great Lakes, it's astounding to see how much pollution comes from those who visit its shores and waters. Pack up what you bring in. Take pride in these great waters and pinch yourself that you are so lucky to be in proximity of such grand nature.

His next answer displayed apprehension. Why were the lakes in trouble when people cared so deeply?

"Sure, some people care deeply. But what good is it if you need to spend so much time fighting with people and politicians who continually believe there are no problems, and who believe climate change is a hoax? Because of this, a great deal of time is spent fending off challenges instead of moving forward."

He had a prescription:

"I think our best hope is educating the young. Today. Not tomorrow."

He was adamant about it. "We need to build a passionate citizenry of young people who are willing to stand up and defend these great waters. The older generations polluted them. The middle generations deny anything is wrong with them. The younger generations must be brought to its shores. They must smell the air. Touch the water."

"Apathy will kill the lakes before anything else ever will."

At first I thought the reference to apathy was a challenge to my assertion that people care deeply about the Lakes. Then it dawned me – millions do care, but they're apathetic about doing anything. Deep down they feel larger forces are in play, and that caring is the end of the road. Action is underwater.

Interlude 20

In his memoir, former Michigan Department of Natural Resources Fisheries Division Chief Howard Tanner remembers the direction given him by the agency's director, Ralph MacMullan, when Tanner took the job. "Do something! And if you can, make it spectacular!" Tanner went on to initiate the planting of Coho and Chinook salmon in the Great Lakes, touching off the sensational growth of a Great Lakes sport fishery with an estimated annual value of $7 to $11 billion. Although some voices have challenged the intentional planting of non-native species in the Great Lakes, none have questioned that what Tanner did was spectacular.

Now it's our turn.

The Great Lakes have fostered many great environmental ideas. But it's perhaps a sign of the political times that the big idea with which they're associated in the political process is money. The Obama Administration's approximately $2 billion Great Lakes Restoration Initiative (GLRI) became a staple of the federal budget. In 2016, the Healing Our Waters coalition, consisting primarily of environmental advocacy groups, challenged presidential candidates to sign onto a platform promising they would recommend funding of at least $300 million each year for GLRI. Surrogates for the two candidates spoke highly of the Lakes but did not talk dollars. The following March, the Trump Administration proposed a 97% cut in GLRI.

The reductions are lamentable, but Great Lakes advocates will never bring home enough money to restore fully such a vast watershed. And even if they could, something would still be lacking. Money can address physical threats and deterioration but can't satisfy spiritual or community needs.

Additionally, the Congressional appropriations game is played by an exclusive club of elected and appointed officials and lobbyists for an array of interests. It does not engage citizens. Sustaining the Great Lakes is not the privilege or duty of the elite. It is the task of all.

What would be something spectacular in the effort to assure healthy, productive and pleasing Great Lakes? Here are a few suggestions:

It would span the U.S-Canadian border.

It would be inclusive of tribes, First Nations and Metis, of all races and faiths and origins.

It would reach into every corner of the Great Lakes ecosystem.

Most of all, it would require something of the citizens of the Great Lakes watershed. More than writing a check to an environmental organization. More than sending an e-mail to a member of Parliament or Congress in support of Great Lakes funding. And more than knowing that pollution is a threat to the health of the Great Lakes.

It would begin with Great Lakes literacy.

A four-year college degree is not needed to be literate in the dynamics of the Great Lakes ecosystem. A citizen need not know what diporeia are but should know the keystone fish species of the Lakes. A citizen need not know what cyanotoxins are but should know that excess phosphorus fosters algae blooms which may contain positions. A citizen need not know what climate change will do to the world but should know what it may do to Great Lakes water levels, water quality, and both native and non-native species. Knowing these things not only enables participation in discussions and decisions affecting the Lakes from Ottawa and Washington, D.C. to the local municipality, but has the potential to increase one's love for these fragile and sublime lakes.

If 10% of the 35 million people knew these things and did something with the knowledge, that would be spectacular.

Chapter 21

One of the last interviews I conducted was of the Grand Old Man of the Great Lakes, Dr. Henry Regier. I knew he would have something important to say. I just wasn't sure I would understand it. Well into his 80s, Henry was still running intellectual rings around me. But I don't think I'm the only one he sometimes baffled.

Henry's Great Lakes CV was as extensive as one of the lakes. After obtaining his bachelor's from Queen's University in 1954 and his Ph.D. from Cornell in 1961, he joined the faculty of the University of Toronto in 1966 as a professor of zoology and eventually also professor of environmental studies. From 1989-94 he was director of the graduate-level, transdisciplinary Institute for Environmental Studies. He worked on both the local and basinwide levels, serving as an ecologist on Toronto area waters beginning in 1954, conducting scientific studies, supervising graduate students, advising colleagues of the Metro Planning Department and the Waterfront Regeneration Trust.

He also took on the larger Great Lakes issues beginning in the mid-1950s, with special focus on Lake Erie. He served as a Canadian commissioner on the Great Lakes Fishery Commission from 1980 to 1989, and on the Great Lakes Science Advisory Board of the International Joint Commission from 1987 to 1990. He received the Centenary Medal of the Royal Society of Canada for co-leadership in a review of the science being done in support of the Great Lakes Water Quality Agreement, the Award of Excellence of the American Fisheries Society and Membership in the Order of Canada, the country's highest civilian honor, in 2008. And there's a lot more.

The journey of this Great Lakes guru began on the Canadian prairies, in Brainerd, Alberta, in 1930. The family moved from Alberta to the Niagara region of Ontario in 1943, one kilometer from Lake Ontario and six kilometers west of the Niagara River.

"The Lake Ontario waters weren't covered with ice but there was a big ridge of broken ice on the narrow beach," Henry wrote to me. "A few meters inland from the beach, a layer of clay about five meters high was eroding and slumping. Several spacious clapboard summer cottages were sliding lakeward. Structurally the summer cottages were of a better quality than any of the self-built log houses in our pioneer settlement in Alberta. I was confused."

I wasn't surprised that instead of answering all of my questions, he found one to be a jumping off point for a theme that had bothered him for a while.

"For the past 19 years," he wrote, "I've been involved with the ostensible remediation of the intense contamination of Canagagigue Creek, and its small basin that includes Elmira [his adopted hometown] as part of the Grand River Basin."

He said a local American-owned chemical plant manufactured materiel for the Canadian and American governments for the world wars, the Korean War, and "the American War on Vietnam." The firm's hazardous wastes were mostly flushed down the creek or dumped into leaky pits in the glacial till within 100 meters of the creek. Henry said landowners were "bought off" through confidential agreements.

When the International Joint Commission's Great Lakes Water Quality Board in the 1980s identified 42 Areas of Concern – highly contaminated rivers, bays and harbors – the company, Henry said, sidestepped the inclusion of its site on the list.

Unhappy with the slow pace of cleanup and the voicelessness of concerned citizens, Henry said he "started a local campaign for a mid-course correction and urged a collaborative approach something like that of the Remedial Action Plans under the Great Lakes Water Quality Board. That revised approach actually got started municipally about three years ago and has mostly been stonewalled by the company and provincial agency."

Henry felt it likely the company and province would continue to make a show of cleaning things up while relying mostly on natural processes to fix things. He was sure that there were numerous contaminated hotspots in the area whose existence all levels of government were trying to conceal.

His cynicism was a sad note. After more than a half century of prize-winning science and advocacy, he mistrusted government. Was there any reason for the rest of us to have confidence in it?

While involved in his community, Henry simultaneously took a broader, planetary view. Henry-isms sprouted.

"From studying a satellite photo of our Great Laurentian Basin, suitably enhanced to note forested regions, I perceive a vast quasi-circular blob starting on the Shield to the northwest and extending to the deciduous forest of the sedimentary Alleghenies to the southeast. This blob is partially intersected with a large tear-drop-shaped, elliptical area that starts on the sedimentary Prairie to the southwest, abuts the Alleghenies and extends northeastward to the Gulf of St. Lawrence. Comparatively, the large mass of waters of northwestern part of the circular NW-to-SE blob are deeper, more lacustrine and naturally nutrient poor and the waters of the elliptical SW-to-NE ellipse are shallower, more riverine and naturally nutrient richer. The vast majority of humans live in the tear-drop blob that is mostly nested in the larger circular blob."

Got that?

With some reason, I thought, Henry carried nostalgia for what he called "the Great Laurentian Spring of 1968-1993," a period when a community of scientists, thinkers and practitioners revolutionized both public understanding of the Lakes' preciousness and the management of the Lakes. In a paper for the *Journal of Great Lakes Research* co-authored with John Jackson and John Coon he said:

"In an absence of any overarching plan or process, numerous commissions at various levels of organizational nesting joined to foster a generation-long self-organizational happening, the Great Laurentian Spring of 1968–93. A series of Canada–US Great Lakes Water Quality Agreements, as overseen by the International Joint Commission (IJC) was accepted as a common focus to which other concerns were then linked. In practice, the mission and strategic plans of the Great Lakes Fishery Commission (GLFC) often served as an effective, if relatively silent, partner especially with respect to innovations. Besides formal government agencies that had links to relevant commissions, university-based researchers in scientific associations, citizens' organizations, industry representatives and occasional churches joined in the complex, semi-chaotic, nested happening or spring-like episode."

"The generation that followed…has soldiered on with much less support from federal governments than during the preceding quarter century."

To my question about the overall trend in the health of the Great Lakes, Henry wrote: "Separate and joint effects of the ten or so major cultural stresses acting on Great Lakes waters have never been assessed as a complex set. I haven't found anyone who has a reliable understanding of how the Great Lakes Basin ecosystem… 'worked' a millennium ago or 'worked' at any time since then. If such a complex assessment could be performed credibly, I suspect that it would yield an inference that the 'health' of Great Lakes waters is getting worse in most of the Basin."

He said there is no one overarching threat to the Great Lakes; the leading problems "would look very different in different locales. The harmful effects or strains due to different stresses tend to have some features that resemble each other and these become complexed autogenously into a general adaptive syndrome, with hideous features. Emergence of [the syndrome] from interaction of effects of more than one stress may be the number one threat."

He referred to an idea that had once intrigued me. A former IJC commissioner had called for a congress of Great Lakes Basin citizens to meet to devise a governance system.

"It could be based on an expansion of a 150-year-old extant epistemic network that could be called the Great Laurentian Network of Basin Ecosystem Researchers," Henry proposed.

One of several reasons the Lakes were in trouble, Henry said, was that "the freedoms that came with the French, American and Russian revolutions brought with them irresponsibilities of various kinds, including with respect to stewarding the 'common property' of valuable nature. Identifying and fencing off large chunks of landscape as parks, reserves, refuges, etc., doesn't compensate effectively."

He signed off self-deprecatingly as Old Deaf Henry, but he could hear the overtones of history far better than me.

Interlude 21

Something about the Great Lakes compels people to make great ventures. A swimmer wonders, "Can I swim across Lake Huron?" A kayaker wonders, "Can I paddle the perimeter of Lake Superior?" And a hiker wonders, "Can I walk the circumference of Lake Michigan?"

Searching for something bigger than themselves – something bigger to do, not just something physically bigger – these daredevils will variously seek to raise money for a worthy cause, win recognition, or peer into their own souls. The quest is not as much about a Great Lake as it is about themselves.

For example:

- *In the summer of 2013, Steve Wargo of South Euclid, Ohio took 19 hours and seven minutes to cross Lake Erie from Long Point, Ontario to Freeport Beach in Pennsylvania. It was a 24.3-mile swim. He became the first Ohioan, the 16th person, and the oldest, at age 55, to make the swim across Lake Erie, according to informal records. Why did he do it? "Because it's there," Wargo said. "Just as a mountain climber looks at mountain, I look at a body of water and say, 'Yeah, I can do that.'" Wargo suffered in his quest: August water temperatures were an unusually low 68 to 72 degrees.*

- *In 2009, Loreen Niewenhuis of Battle Creek, Michigan walked 1,019 miles around Lake Michigan, often on the water's exact fringe. She did it in ten segments with breaks between. She wrote a book about it,* A 1000-Mile Walk on the Beach *(and later books about other Great Lakes treks.) Why did she do it? "The nest was emptying," she told a reporter. "But I felt I could stack up novels and not have an agent and be in my office writing novels forever. So I thought, let me do something completely different and get out of my office." She added, more mystically, "There is something about being where water meets land. I feel very clicked-in there. I feel like I can go forever."*

- *In the summer of 2015, Jared Munch of Duluth, Minnesota piloted his stand-up paddleboard approximately 1,350 miles along the shoreline of Lake Superior. Then 23 years old, he was raising money for a neighborhood youth services program – by being the first person to use such a paddleboard to tour the lake. He suffered, too. "It's not the physical fatigue wearing me out," he said. "It's the mental fatigue of being on the lake so long and stuck in the same routine over and over, paddling 30 or 40 miles of flat water every day. It's not the most exciting thing, but I'm getting it done."*

Then there is the separate category of motorized attempts to humble the Great Lakes. Not consciously, but humble nonetheless. Rumor has it a motorcyclist once rode the 1400-mile circle tour of Lake Superior in 24 hours – a little like devouring a banquet in 60 seconds. Better documented are the madhouse bids to see, or swim in all five Great Lakes in a day.

Kathryn Kinville and Shelby Kear summarized their May 2012 trek this way: "Two friends, 15 hours of driving, 882 miles, swimming in all five Great Lakes in one day! Mission Complete!"

There's poignancy in all of these journeys. In those propelled by muscles rather than motors, the point seems to be challenging one's physical and mental boundaries while becoming intimate with the Great Lakes in a way you can't in a day or a drive-by. In the others, the point seems chiefly a novelty or a conversation piece. But a single thread does link them – the desire to be great, even for just one day.

Can we strive to be great in care of the Great Lakes instead of just great in our quest to challenge them?

Chapter 22

I don't recall exactly how I heard of Paul Parks or he of me, but I recall *him* vividly. Passion is difficult to forget.

He was passionate about his family, I know. And his cottage. But he was passionate about the cottage in part because it overlooked his beloved Lake Michigan. When he sensed a threat to that lake this compact man reared up like a grizzly.

The threat was directional drilling for oil and gas under Lake Michigan. Also known as slant drilling, it's a technique for extracting these under-the-lake hydrocarbons from an onshore wellhead.

Having witnessed oil spills in America's oceans, with the attendant carnage of marine life, the public and its policymakers wanted nothing similar to foul the Great Lakes. In 1982, the Michigan Legislature had enacted a ban on oil drilling in the Lakes. Most people assumed that was the end of it.

They were wrong.

The state ban prohibited drilling in the Lakes, not drilling *under* the Lakes from shore. The difference, according to the cavalier command of the state Department of Environmental Quality (DEQ), was that directional drilling posed virtually no risk. There was no reason to ban it.

On the other side, Great Lakes advocates challenged the safety assurances of the DEQ bureaucrats. They cited numerous previous examples of supposedly foolproof technologies that caused catastrophic environmental damage. Further, why take even an insignificant risk given the minor benefit? The estimate of recoverable oil under Lake Michigan was a supply that would last the nation two to three weeks.

Tilting as usual toward resource exploitation, the DEQ, under the direction of Governor John Engler, announced in February 2001 that the state would terminate a moratorium and begin offering leases for slant drilling under the Great Lakes. Only the oil and gas industry seemed enthusiastic about that; and of those who were most distressed by the decision, Paul Parks stood out. We talked, we commiserated, and I drove from Lansing to Grand Haven to meet him.

Paul was not well. He looked – and I'm sure he knew he looked – in decline. But he treated me as an honored guest. The honor was real. Seeing him *and* Lake Michigan was a godsend. I remember a man deeply outraged by the idea that public officials would ransom the Great Lakes for less than a month's worth of oil. He simply couldn't believe it. And as he spoke, I became mesmerized by his conviction.

"My father didn't believe in God or the stock market," his daughter wrote me years later. "He believed in the state of Michigan and in the Great Lakes. The former as the home of his ancestors—copper miners, ship builders, teachers—and the latter because they represented everything in his life that was true. Everything that was noble. Everything right, pure, lovely, admirable, excellent, and praiseworthy. Michigan and the Great Lakes were his religion: he drew his comfort and meaning from them. He came by this honestly, as his parents and grandparents held these same beliefs."

The cottage was *Fleur de Lis,* named by the Chicago family that built it in 1905. The cottage came into the Parks' possession in 1921. Paul's mother took ownership in 1927. Mary wrote, "Depression wiped out her inheritance. The last piece of property she still owned was *Fleur de Lis.* Though it was double mortgaged, she refused to let it go, renting it out in the summertime to keep the mortgage interest and taxes paid. For many years, she and her family were only able make brief visits to the cottage during the off-season. This made my father's time there more precarious and more precious. When he was a teenager in the 1930s, Dad would shovel his way into the cottage through snow or wind-blown sand and camp out with only the fireplace and lanterns for light."

Ultimately, the Parks' finances stabilized, and the family was able to enjoy entire summers at *Fleur de Lis.* Wrote Mary, "My father's closest friends were the kids he met from the other cottages on Stickney Ridge. There was always swimming and boating and bonfires. Swing music jounced his parents' Victrola. When the lake water level was low the young men would play baseball in front of the cottage and the young women would smoke and tan and cheer them on."

Paul met his wife-to-be on a blind date in 1938. *Fleur de Lis* hosted their wedding reception five years later. The family wandered across the continent but Paul never lost his attachment to the cottage. In 1970, the family moved into it.

Mary remembers earthy conditions at *Fleur de Lis.* Everything from the paned windows to the plumbing needed frequent work, but Paul's engineering degree equipped him well to assure the cottage was functional shelter.

Paul told me he habitually observed the lake from a lookout in front of the cottage, where he could follow the weather and freighter traffic. Mary added that the lookout was a favorite spot for him to read newspapers, listen to the Coast Guard on radio, and watch his beloved Chicago Cubs on a portable TV.

He taught his four children to swim and to sail in the "Big Lake." Family vacations were spent in a 1950s-era wooden Chris-Craft cabin cruiser, harbor hopping up the coast to Whitehall, Frankfort, the Straits, the Soo, and once as far north as Tahquamenon.

Paul was in his 80s when the state government announced it would resume leasing under the Great Lakes. He heard about it from Mary, who called him at the cottage after listening to an interview conducted by Shelley Irwin, the host of the local public radio station's morning show.

Paul lobbied the old-fashioned way. Using a manual typewriter, he manufactured an impressive number of letters. But he adapted quickly to modern technology when his children bought him a TV-based Internet connection.

Mary observed, "His emails were unmistakable—terse, to the point, often lacking pronouns or articles. Always a clear and forceful writer, he added his 50+ years of engineering expertise to the debate. 'Nothing man makes is infallible,' he would write. 'Risk analysis never takes in the true cost of an environmental disaster. Why should private companies have the right to risk the health of the Lakes? For a few lousy bucks?'"

He didn't just write letters. He also spoke out at public meetings convened by the city, county and DEQ. That's probably where he made the greatest difference. A little over 5 feet tall, but with a firm voice, Paul was a special asset to the battle.

Ultimately, the public delivered a victory for Paul's Lake Michigan and the other Lakes. The clamor was impossible for legislators to ignore in an election year. Rejecting the pleadings of a governor of their own party, legislative Republicans joined Democrats in approving legislation placing a statutory ban on directional drilling. A truculent Engler neither signed the ban nor vetoed it. He let it become law without his signature, under a relatively obscure provision of the state constitution.

Paul was not able to celebrate long. His health went downhill.

"The day he died in a local nursing home," Mary wrote, "he'd been barely conscious most of the day. When we asked him if he knew where he was, he answered the question patiently as if the answer were obvious: "Of course I know where I am. I'm at the cottage, where else would I be?"

Interlude 22

It's a truism of life that you can be so familiar with something that you don't recognize it anymore. It could be a marriage partner with whom you've spent years who suddenly surprises you with undiscovered gifts. It can be a job that abruptly calls on you to summon and express new talent. Or it can be a body of water that you have lived beside as you might live beside a heavily trafficked road and block out the sound.

For me it was the St. Clair River. Technically a strait roughly 39 miles long connecting Lake Huron with Lake St. Clair, it feels more like a canal as it begins. Ridiculously narrow for an indispensable natural pipeline for ecology and world commerce, the St. Clair River has its charms.

I came to see them more clearly when my younger brother made a 200-mile round trip to Port Huron on Christmas Eve Day with two objectives:(1) to dine at a favorite Mexican restaurant; and (2) to walk beside the St. Clair. I was impressed. What was it about the river that appealed to him beyond the basics? The open horizon of Lake Huron just to the north commanded my fascination and delivered peace.

We finished the meal at his chosen restaurant, then drove down near the footing of the Blue Water Bridge, parked, and began walking along the St. Clair in the gathering dusk. What immediately came to our attention was the soothing sound of gently swirling water. It was as refreshing to hear as a glass of cold clean water is refreshing to taste on a punishingly hot summer day.

As we took our first strides to the north, one of the season's last freighters came around the bend in the shoreline toward us. The slightly defaced lettering on the bow identified it as the Algoma Equinox. It seemed to hurry, raw winter chasing it from the upper lakes. We turned around, watching the immense freighter race away down the constricted river. A wingless jumbo jet taxiing down a Manhattan thoroughfare would look no more incongruous.

We conversed about various subjects, but the river was the unifying thread. We mused on the difference between the nearly abandoned riverside parking lots on December 24 and the overflow in the same lots in July and August. The lack of river lovers this day was no surprise, but I was finding that an hour's walk along the St. Clair, even on a blustery December day, was worth rising from the couch.

My brother looked to the residences on the opposing side of the road from our walkway and said enthusiastically, "In 10 or 15 years some of these will be gone and there'll be 10-story apartment buildings with great views just like on the Canadian side." I shared his enthusiasm for making the St. Clair more accessible but not for lining the western bank of the river with high-rises. Still, he had grasped the appeal of this place, this river, before I had.

We took other trips along the river. We journeyed south one day to the City of St. Clair, a pleasant community with a long ribbon of park along the river. We wanted to see the St. Clair Inn, where our parents had spent many wedding anniversaries watching the freighters pass by. Now shuttered due to bankruptcy, it seemed a relic, but rumors of its reopening and remodeling persisted.

The small city also made a big claim: that it contained the longest freshwater boardwalk in the world. We explored it. The claim was, well, charming. The larger point is that the community embraced the river as my brother did. The city's enthusiasm was partially rooted in money but it opened the river up to more and more people, and ultimately might generate more Great Lakes defenders.

There's far more to the river that I haven't seen. It terminates in a mammoth delta which has long been recognized as a hunting and fishing dream. As I continue to explore I'll keep in mind the word mystery: no part of the Great Lakes system is fully known and each part is a source of wonder.

Like the St. Marys, the Detroit, and the Niagara, the St. Clair is more than an afterthought of nature; it's a vital artery. We don't fall in love with human arteries, but those that pump fresh water deserve, at least, our respect.

Summing Up: Part 1

Where do all these memories, emotions, reflections, judgments and speculations leave us?

For me, the answer is in uncertainty, bordering on anxiety.

My friends and colleagues all recovered early and mostly fond memories of one of the Great Lakes and expressed their deep attachment to these sacred places. But a few of them also offered novel explanations for the floundering health of the Lakes that I hadn't considered.

It shocks no one to say that between the citizenry and the government, especially in the U.S., is a gulf of cynicism and contempt that interferes with the formation of policies. It is not headline news that business interests that would have to pay more for cleaner Great Lakes will oppose any such requirements, and typically prevail.

It's not original, either, to observe that Americans spend less time outdoors and more time sucking at the fire hose of entertainment in their smart phones and computers, and therefore are less aware of and less engaged with the environment generally, including the Great Lakes.

A familiar theme of the aggregated interviews is that perceived responsibility for protecting the Great Lakes is diffused among many agencies and levels of government. And not all the parties mentioned have any management powers. I worked for one such institution, the International Joint Commission, identified in several interviews. The IJC assesses and reports on the progress of governments in meeting the goals of the Great Lakes Water Quality Agreement, but its role on the issue is wholly advisory. When everyone is responsible, no one is responsible. And when advisors are thought to be managers, the real managers escape responsibility.

Perhaps Tracey Easthope had properly characterized a major cause of the problem: sheer complexity. So many factors contributed to the decline of the Lakes, so many different agencies and institutions had a piece of the action in restoring them, that the public was flummoxed. This was a crystallization of already available wisdom.

But it startled me to hear a suggestion that Michiganders living 50 miles away from a Great Lake might not think of them often. Growing up in the state, I always assumed the Great Lakes were a cherished part of every Michiganders' inheritance. But as I tested the hypothesis out on others – including inlanders – I found agreement.

An Ann Arbor friend was the first to make the point. She was not convinced that people do care so much about the Great Lakes. She doubted landlocked people in the state care or think about them often. She said the Huron River, which rolls through the area, is much more on the minds of the Ann Arbor community.

Then there was the difference among communities according to lake. I noticed that in the International Joint Commission public opinion survey, a slightly higher percentage of respondents from the Lake Superior watershed perceived deterioration than did respondents from the Lake Erie watershed. That was counterintuitive. I asked a friend and longtime citizen leader on Great Lakes protection, Jane Elder why that might be true.

"When you live in the Lake Superior region," Jane wrote, "you are very aware that you are in Lake Superior Country. Folks in the UP get the moods, the big water, the weather, the wildlife and fish. It is a more rural and small town population. It is part of your culture and identity.

"In suburban Ohio, how many people see themselves as living in 'Lake Erie country,' unless you are on the shore? Maybe they go to Cedar Point on a weekend in the summer, or are bummed for their Aunt Lucy whose drinking water was yucky a year ago, but Lake Erie doesn't define their sense of place across a region in the way that Superior does.

"When we were in Bayfield last summer, we picked up a T-shirt that says, 'The Lake is the Boss.' Anyone who lives in Superior country gets that. Someone from Lansing, or even Cleveland probably wouldn't identify with that same connection and awareness."

Jane's insight reminded me, however, that just as all politics is local, all Great Lakes issues are local. My interviewees tended to profess concern for the Lakes as a whole, but that was not typical, no matter how much I wanted to believe so. Perhaps the Lakes suffered because many couldn't see the forest for the seas. Systems are abstractions for any mind. A water panorama in front of you is wordless poetry for any heart.

It rattled my cage of assumptions, too, when my wise friend in Liverpool, Sarah Clement, said that the environmental values professed by so many in both quantitative and qualitative reviews of public opinion may be skin deep. Perhaps, she said, people tell pollsters that they care for the lakes because it's something they feel obligated to express, given that voices all around them also express the sentiment. They may not feel as strongly as we assume they do, she said. "Maybe it's just the same as so many other behaviors. We all know we should eat more vegetables, exercise, and drive less, but most of us don't do these things."

After considering her ideas, I felt foolish. She was right. And I had been living in the comforting womb of wishful thinking.

I expressed the most fervent of these wishes in one of my writings. Lighthouse fanatics, freighter lovers, shipwreck enthusiasts, anglers, boaters, divers, swimmers and others could unite in a powerful force that would rescue the Lakes from indifferent or craven lawmakers, I wrote. They "could show the world" how to protect an ecosystem. But whom had I been kidding? Myself, most of all.

There's a reason why there are so many Great Lakes factions. These communities of interest do not see the same thing when they look at the water. Equally important, they bring starkly different values, interests and life experiences to their corner of the Lakes. They share a physical but not an emotional geography. Other than the draining of the Great Lakes, it is difficult to imagine a threat that would unite these communities in common cause to defend them.

And what about the role of individuals in saving the Great Lakes? Some whom I had interviewed were optimists. Brenda Archambo, the "Sturgeon General" of northeast Lower Michigan, was one. "For the most part, people care and if you educate and engage them we will pressure decision makers and make policy changes," she said.

Tony Infante had put it harshly but compellingly: "We continue to avoid making the changes and investments required to restore the health of the Great Lakes…the Great Lakes continue to provide humans with enough benefits that we won't care until enough people understand how our abuse of the ecosystem impacts our health or rapacious consumption."

In a similar vein, Daniel Macfarlane, a Canadian-born scholar and assistant professor of freshwater policy at Western Michigan University, observed that "people may say they 'value' the Great Lakes, but that may well mean that they value the economic activity it supports. They may say they want the Great Lakes protected, but when it comes to a choice between environment and economics, the latter tends to win.

"We're addicted to growth in this country," he said. "The Grand Canyon was almost flooded, Niagara Falls was almost turned off – no natural icon is safe when there is money to be made. A spill on Line 5 [twin oil pipelines crossing the Straits of Mackinac] might be horrible – but people are willing to ignore and look the other way since they are reliant on fossil fuels."

And who am I to criticize? I drive a car, often long distances. I take long, hot showers. I use ample electricity – to write this book, for example. That's all concrete. If I had any beneficial influence on the Great Lakes through policy, it was diffused and immeasurable.

But there had also been, and continued to be, people like Paul Parks. Just one man – old, frail, but animated by an unhesitating devotion to Lake Michigan and willing to exhaust himself in its defense. He had made a difference. He had helped prevent one threat. What was the difference between Paul and other people that Tony described?

Place – Fleur de Lis on the Lake Michigan shore in Paul's case and all the memories cultivated there – had something to do with it. But everyone I had interviewed referred to memories associated with a Great Lakes place. Some superior spark propelled Paul differently. Not a professional or even seasoned amateur lobbyist, he had put aside retirement and become compelling voice for the lake.

I was sure there were similar true hearts across the watershed. Together, they were the proverbial sleeping giant. Why hadn't they arisen like Paul?

Summing Up: Part II

The search for a cure to the problems of the Great Lakes will go on as long as there are vulnerable lakes and fallible humans. But those humans made progress in improving the health of the Lakes for over 40 years beginning around 1970. Further progress, if not perfection, is possible.

But how? There is no one answer. There may be several overarching answers, however.

While dining with Michigan Technological University professors Nancy and Martin Auer on a visit to campus, I learned of an unusual piece they and colleagues had published in *The Journal of Great Lakes Research*. It was not quantitative. It did not include methods and results. It was almost a plea.

Their first message was that the Great Lakes are facing "an end game scenario." In part, they wrote, this was the result of a popular belief in the Great Lakes as "infinite and ever resilient" and the consequences: "trillions of mussels distributed over millions of hectares of lake bottom, unprecedented loads of bioavailable phosphorus delivered from highly agricultural watersheds and increased volumes of human effluents and a toxic substance, mercury, the management of which is opposed by many for economic and energy policy reasons, and more."

The remedy, they submitted, was a new way of thinking and caring. "The people living within the Great Lakes Basin must come together and begin to deeply believe that these waters and all their ecological connections are a Commons: an entire ecosystem on which we depend, if we want life therein to survive and thrive. Humankind finds itself at a critical juncture; we need to begin to make radically different personal, management and governing choices than we have, if we want to sustain the planet and our lives and those of generations to come."

It was easy to agree with their observation that public policy and regulation would not improve without much greater public participation. Instead, they declared, the Basin lacked "sufficient community outcry and action to provide the catalyst necessary to change course."

I had not before seen the noun "reverence" used in a science journal, but the authors said that attitude was necessary if a policy and management course correction was to occur.

"We must recognize that the Great Lakes are a gift and a responsibility 'held in common' by the peoples and communities of the Lakes. On a second level, humankind must come together as a community, as representatives of that Commons, bringing reverence, knowledge, experience and insight to bear on matters of Great Lakes management and governance. It is of value to the Commoners to realize that their voice matters and that their actions are vital to how we care for the Lakes, the entire ecosystem and its connection to the whole Earth."

All right, then. I could not disagree – except with the realism, or lack of same, in expecting such a transformation of consciousness any time soon. I had once believed that such a transformation was imminent, or at least would happen in my lifetime. No more.

I knew of another idea – a tool that, if wielded correctly, could both precipitate and capitalize on a new mental framework for the millions. But while pragmatic, it is almost unknown to the populace. It is the public trust doctrine. Legendary environmental attorney Jim Olson schooled me on it.

An element of common law reaching back to the Romans, the public trust doctrine is based on the physical reality that some natural resources, including the sea, the lands beneath them and immediately adjacent shoreline, do not lend themselves to private ownership. Rather, they are forever to be held in trust by government for present and future generations. In the United States, both the U.S. and several state supreme courts have found in favor of those seeking to enforce the doctrine to prevent state transfer of submerged lands, including those under Great Lakes, to private parties.

In practice, however, government regulators are loath to invoke the doctrine in decision-making, seeming to view it as a policy statement without weight rather than a centuries-old rule with the gravitas of countless generations of precedent. That is circular reasoning. If it is not used, it has no weight. Governments need to use it and citizens need to demand it.

How could it transform protection of the Great Lakes? By reminding the public that the collective "we" own the Lakes, and that no private party has the right to impair them. This shifts the burden from the government to the applicant who wants to use of the waters or submerged lands. He, she or it must demonstrate no substantial impairment of the public trust. If such an impairment is likely to occur, the trustee acting on behalf of the public – our government – must deny the proposed use. Similar principles exist in Canadian common law.

This could stop a corporate leviathan from appropriating large amounts of Great Lakes Basin water for sale and private profit, or eject the Straits of Mackinac pipelines for violation of the terms of an easement to use the public's submerged lands for the crossing. It might even force a reduction of the phosphorus pollution impairing public uses of western Lake Erie. That's the point – the power of the public trust doctrine is sure, and could be vast.

Think of the Lakes as a commons, per the suggestion of the Auers and colleagues, but back it up with legal force. That might make a difference.

The first book about the Great Lakes that I read was authored by William Ashworth. Published in 1986, *The Late Great Lakes* told a story consistent with its title. Victims of unrelenting abuse since the Europeans arrived, the Lakes weren't just dying, they were almost if not already dead.

But the book wasn't really the downer that it appeared. Implicit in Ashworth's effort was a belief that the Lakes could yet be saved. He seemed not to be writing an obituary as much as an appeal. Like Scrooge on Christmas Eve, we still had time to make things right.

Unfortunately, those who didn't read the book might have drawn conclusions from its title: another woe-is-me tale of gloom and doom from an environmentalist. If things were so bad, why bother doing anything about the Great Lakes?

Eighteen years later I wrote a book titled *On the Brink: The Great Lakes in the 21st Century*. The title was a conscious attempt at duality. I've heard people say that something is on the brink of disaster, and I've heard people say that someone is on the brink of stardom – or greatness. But based on the reaction I've received, I'm one of the few who's used "on the brink" as a prefix to something good.

Let me be clear: I am optimistic about the future of the Great Lakes, and the nation of people who know and benefit from them. But I am not a Pollyanna. We in the Lake Nation will have to make difficult choices, and sacrifices, to assure the greatness of the Lakes into the future. This is something no politician will ever tell you. But it is a fact.

For what can be dearer to us, besides lovers, family and friends, than our experience and memory of place?

On a group camping trip to Horseshoe Bay in far northwest Lake Huron, after a savory meal, someone suggested going down to the water again. Once we reached the shoreline, I decided to head south, while three or four others trekked to the north.

It would soon be a blue night. The sun had plunged behind the coastal forest well before. As I finished my short hike, I turned around. Under a pale lake of sky, beside silver waters, my comrades were tiny figures kicking stones, dipping their toes in the water, and enjoying laughter barely audible from my distance. For some reason I can't quite fathom, decades later that scene remains engraved in memory.

On a trip home from Washington, D.C. to Lansing, Michigan, a friend and I decided to take the long route – the *very* long route -- through Pennsylvania and New York to see Lake Ontario. We left America's capital at mid-afternoon that August day and drove madly on interstates and two-lanes. The sun outpaced us. Yet somehow the light of day lingered just long enough to reach Lakeside State Park, west of Rochester. Flags snapped in the wind against a darkening sky while waves thundered against the shore. We listened to it appreciatively for 10 minutes. It was worth all the effort.

After participating in a meeting about Lake Erie's sickening algal blooms at Maumee Bay State Park in November 2014, I wandered out to the water's edge. At night, and at that time of year, algae are not to be seen. For all my senses told me, the lake was as it always had been. A fitful wind stirred the water into lyrics. They sang of grandeur past and to come. The lake would rebound.

If given a chance.

Postscript

February 19, 2017. Yesterday I saw the first barefoot print of the year in the beach sand. There were many other shoeprints and boot prints and paw prints. The walk took longer because Fitz wanted to sniff all of the indentations made by dogs, and also because the calm, warm air relaxed my habitual desire to move on.

Enjoying spring-like weather more than a month before spring is said to begin – and two months before you can somewhat depend on it in southern Lower Michigan – is a guilty pleasure. While exulting in the freedom from gloves, hats and thick coats, a few friends say the weather is disorienting. Something is wrong, they say. Nature is out of its reassuring cycle.

The temperature climbed to 68 degrees yesterday, over 30 degrees above average.

But I remember conditions during exactly the same week two years ago, when I visited here. The temperature was in the minus teens when I arrived in the middle of the night. Two feet of snow smothered the land. Lake Huron appeared completely ice-covered from this vantage point. The Great Lakes as a whole were over 90% ice-covered. Right now, the figure is less than 10%. The point is that any single stretch of weather says little. Yet our hearts hear an emphatic message.

The beach during this intermission from winter is different from the beach in summer. Built up by wave action during colder weather, two parallel ridges of sand remain after the ice mounds beneath them have melted.

In the afternoon light, a stripe of white appeared far out on the lake. I believe it was a last stray ice floe trying to evade destruction. By evening I imagine it met its demise, for I could no longer spot it.

It is an odd time in the world when weather so fair should seem so ominous.

Appendix
The Fundamental Five

Every patriot is expected to know the history of his or her nation and its system of governance. In the de facto Lake Nation, every patriot should know five things in five categories about the five Great Lakes. This list is one person's idea; experts can and do have their own lists, many based on extensive grounding in science and/or environmental education.

Freshwater Facts
- Only freshwater will sustain human life.
- About 97% of the water on earth is salt water.
- Of the remaining fraction of approximately 3% that is freshwater, over 98% is locked in ice caps, glaciers and groundwater.
- Of the remaining fraction of about 1.2% of all freshwater, about .25% is found at the surface in lakes and streams.
- The Great Lakes contain almost 20% of that .25% – one-fifth of all available surface freshwater in the world.[1]

Great Lakes Volume and Transit Facts
- The Great Lakes contain 95% of the surface water volume of the United States.
- The Great Lakes contain 84% of the surface water volume of North America.
- Only 1% of the volume of the Great Lakes is renewed annually from precipitation and runoff; the water balance of the Lakes is delicate.
- The average drop of water takes 173 years to pass through Lake Superior.
- The average drop of water takes 204 years to pass from Lake Superior to the ocean.

[1] You will find slightly different figures in different sources, demonstrating the inexactness of much of our knowledge about the Great Lakes. The Great Lakes Information Network (http://www.great-lakes.net/lakes/ref/lakefact.html) pegs the total at about one-fifth, US EPA (https://www.epa.gov/greatlakes/great-lakes-facts-and-figures) at about 21%, and Environment and Climate Change Canada (https://www.ec.gc.ca/grandslacs-greatlakes/default.asp?lang=En&n=3F5214D0-1) say it's 18%.

Environmental Problem Facts
- More than 180 invasive and non-native species, including the zebra and quagga mussel, have disrupted the ecology of the Great Lakes.
- Although government bans and pollution prevention programs have reduced levels of toxic substances like DDT and PCBs in Great Lakes fish and wildlife, newly introduced chemicals and mercury pose significant risks.
- Agricultural runoff is the leading source of phosphorus pollution fostering harmful algal blooms in Lake Erie, Saginaw Bay and Green Bay.
- All 107 water samples collected from 29 Great Lakes tributaries in Minnesota, Wisconsin, Indiana, Michigan, Ohio and New York for a 2016 study contained microplastics. Microplastics come from decomposing bottles and bags, wear off synthetic clothing and at one time were manufactured into some personal care products.
- Continued population growth in the Southwestern United States is leading to freshwater scarcity that could increase demand for Great Lakes water.

Political Facts
- Eight states and Ontario border the Great Lakes; Quebec is included in many Great Lakes governance processes because it receives the outflow from the Lakes.
- Michigan is the only state entirely within the Great Lakes watershed.[2]
- The eight Great Lakes states have adopted a legal compact banning most diversions of water outside the basin, but Congress can repeal this at its discretion.
- Six of the eight Great Lakes states are expected to lose seats in the U.S. House of Representatives in 2020, further eroding the region's voting power in Congress.
- No one international, federal, interstate or provincial government has lead authority or coordinating powers to manage the Great Lakes.

Fun Facts
- Spread evenly across the 48 contiguous states, the Great Lakes would turn the U.S. into a swimming pool 9.5 feet deep.

[2] Two tiny portions of Michigan along the Upper Peninsula border with Wisconsin and the Lower Peninsula border with Indiana drain to the Mississippi.

- There are approximately 35,000 islands in the Great Lakes, including the largest lake island in the world, Manitoulin.
- There are about 10,900 miles of Great Lakes shoreline, 200 miles less than the distance between Detroit and Perth, Australia.
- Measured by surface area, Lake Superior is the largest freshwater lake in the world, Lake Huron is third, Lake Michigan is fourth, Lake Erie is tenth and Lake Ontario is twelfth.
- Lake Superior could contain all the other Great Lakes plus three more lakes the size of Lake Erie.

Made in the USA
Lexington, KY
03 November 2018